Advance Praise

"Mr. Marble hasn't just ~~r~~ leadership.
At the core, he ~~'~~ ~~h~~at is both
relatable yet ins ~~Maize~~ will
create a moment awareness for its
readers by being re ~~princ~~ially didactic."
—**~~D~~ave Kipe**, Chief Operating Officer

"All leaders create a personal journey as they navigate their work experiences throughout their lives. Mr. Marble's book *The Monkey and The Maize* challenges the reader to not only reflect on their personal journey, but to compartmentalize the lessons they have learned along the way. As a female leader, this book also pushed me to acknowledge the traits I value and respect and hopefully model in my organization through my words and actions."
—**Dr. Gretchen Guitard**, Superintendent/
College Professor

"My friend Steve Marble is the most deliberately contemplative corporate leader I know, and I'm truly thankful he has distilled his decades of lessons learned into this extended leadership parable. Readers will be encouraged and inspired to imitate Steve's disciplines of daily pursuing wisdom, making relationships central, embracing rigorous work and hard decisions, and keeping a sense of wonder along the way."
—**Colonel Eric R Bents**, USAF (Ret)

"*The Monkey and the Maize* will bring out the emotion of each reader in a different way. The simplicity allows the reader to illustrate images in their mind of the adventures of Pete the monkey. This book is an invaluable resource on leadership and servanthood. I loved every word of it."

—**Michelle Clark**, Site Leader

"Mr. Marble's book is magnificent, encapsulating the principles of knowledge, experience and fortitude, the fundamental foundation of western civilization throughout the ages. Paralleling Greek philosophy, his reflections teach readers the value of knowing thyself and being of sound mind and body as they encounter adversity and success. Most importantly, we find that foundation is based upon faith, family and friends."

—**Jerry Westbrook**, Dean of Students, Associate Vice Chancellor of Student Affairs, Professor of Education, Director Career Planning & Placement (retired) (University of Mississippi, University of Arkansas, University of Chicago, and Southeast Missouri State University)

The Monkey and the Maize

THE Monkey AND THE Maize

AN ALLEGORICAL TALE OF
DEVELOPING LEADERSHIP SKILLS
IN BUSINESS AND IN LIFE

S. Mosby Marble

NEW YORK

LONDON • NASHVILLE • MELBOURNE • VANCOUVER

The Monkey and the Maize

An Allegorical Tale of Developing Leadership Skills in Business and in Life

Published in New York, New York, by Morgan James Publishing. Morgan James is a trademark of Morgan James, LLC. www.MorganJamesPublishing.com

ISBN 9781631952609 paperback
ISBN 9781631952616 eBook
Library of Congress Control Number: 2020940585

Cover and Interior Design by:
Chris Treccani
www.3dogcreative.net

Editor: David Lambert

Cover Image: 588ku from pngtree.com

Morgan James is a proud partner of Habitat for Humanity Peninsula and Greater Williamsburg. Partners in building since 2006.

Get involved today! Visit
MorganJamesPublishing.com/giving-back

To Elaina, "Ellie," my wife and best friend
for more than three decades, whose grace and
courage through numerous battles with cancer
inspired me to write this story.

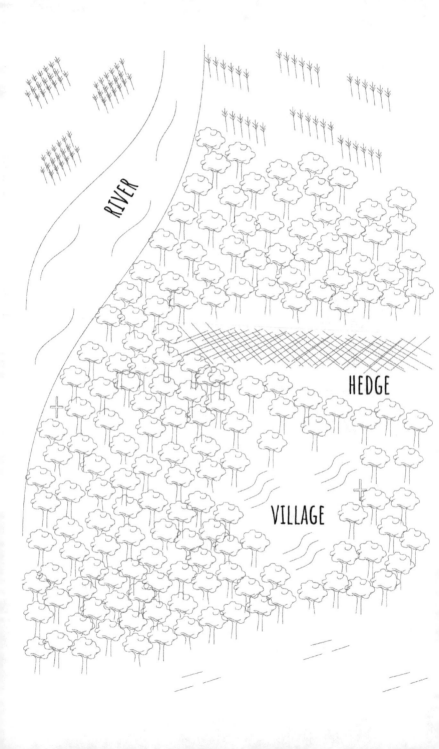

RIVER

HEDGE

VILLAGE

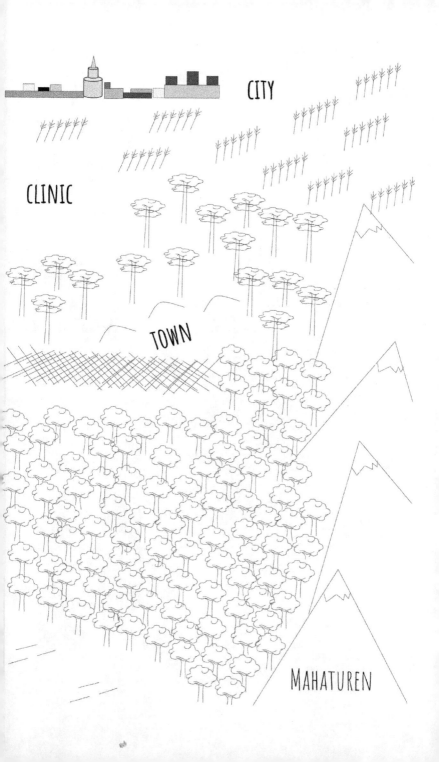

Introduction

Staring at my reflection on the surface of cold coffee in a paper cup, I realized this was a pivotal moment in my life's story, with an outcome entirely out of my control. It had taken more than fifty years of what had seemed to be an average life to lead me here.

It was late on a Thursday night, or possibly very early the next morning—I'm not sure. My best friend and wife of more than thirty years was lying in an operating room somewhere in this massive medical institution. After years of battling cancer and enduring lengthy surgeries, she was unexpectedly in critical condition, and the outlook was not promising. We had made the two-hour trip together, but now I sat alone. What we had expected to be a simple procedure to prepare her for further treatment had become far more complicated, and now, without warning, I was facing the reality that she might not come home.

My sixteen-year-old son would be playing football in the state playoffs the next day, but the anticipation we had all felt about that milestone had evaporated. In its place, I felt a deep coldness.

Closing my eyes in silent prayer, I reflected on my children, my siblings, and my parents. Both of my parents were deceased, but at that moment their faces were as real to me as if they were in the room. My parents' strong faith had not only helped them to overcome adversity but also enabled them to help many others. They had poured their hearts into me. Staring into my cold coffee that night, I realized that none of us succeed alone.

And just as I and many others had benefited from the efforts of my parents, I realized that night that perhaps others would benefit from my story.

My life is not remarkable, and my accomplishments are not necessarily noteworthy. The things that are extraordinary are the people I have been fortunate to meet along my journey, the lessons I have learned, and the principles that tie them all together. Thirty years of leadership in community, entrepreneurship, and corporate positions all pointed to the same recipe. There are roots that sustain, unite, and balance us through life's journey.

Being raised in the woods of southwest Missouri introduced me to those roots early in life. I became an astute observer, valuing success and failure equally. Discipline sustained me in various roles: school board member, adjunct instructor at a community college, member of nonprofit boards of director, and serving as a deacon in my church. My career has been dedicated to maximizing customer experience and leading people. Owning and operating a dry-cleaner and laundry taught me the value of hard work and knowing my customer. Leading large support teams in a corporate setting extended those lessons to invest in the development of others.

I wrote this story from the imaginary forest of my childhood. I recall, as early as elementary school, climbing the trees near our home and resting on their limbs to process life. It was safe. To me, it was more than a tract of woodland—it was a storybook land, a place where spectacular animals came to life and aided my journey through the challenges of adolescence. When I became an adult, that storybook forest receded to a distant memory, but its peace remained. But on that night in the hospital, facing the possibility that my life would change in profound and unsettling ways, I recalled those flights of imagination in that soothing setting, and recalled also how the wisdom I discovered there helped me find the courage to find and to trust my path in life.

Now I offer this story, my fantastic forest, and this cast of colorful characters to serve as a guide or champion within your own story—as a safe setting to embrace the unique cast of characters in your own life, in your community, and among those who serve as leaders. My hope is that my years of relationships and responsibility will bring this fictional story to life for those who want to grow in leadership within their community and their areas of influence at any level. It attempts to weave values and principles into the lives of the characters—which are based on my life.

This story describes a pathway, not a directive. My hope is that each reader will see their own life reflected in this journey and identify with many of the challenges and successes these characters experience. Life presents each of us with so many opportunities to build community. My hope is that each reader of this book will, afterward, be better able to grow their roots, face their hedge, finish strong—and find their best self along the way.

So grab a cup of coffee and join Pete in our shared journey!

Chapter One

Deep in the night, in the flickering candlelight, my aging face reflected in the antique mirror. Sleepless hours, now my unrelenting adversary, taunted me with the gravity of my situation. The crevices in my face represented years of stress from a life of obligation I could no longer either endure or afford. Why hadn't I seen this coming? Where had I gone wrong?

"What are you going to do?" I whispered to the weakened face staring back at me.

Seeking temporary relief, I thought back to a simpler time …

I was a young boy. Very young. The air was bitterly cold, but pride warmed me. Before me stood a mountain of a man. To me he seemed as tall as a mighty oak. He wore an orange hat, orange vest, and had a shotgun calmly resting on his shoulder. This was my first foray into the wilds to hunt. Gripping the hickory stick that served as my rifle for the day, I leapt after him on the trail, placing my feet directly in the impressions left by his boots. I loved every minute of this time with him.

"Are you OK?" My wife's voice startled me back to reality.

Part of the burden of responsibility is knowing when to include those you love in the magnitude of a situation. Although she was an invaluable sounding board and counselor, tonight was a solo flight. "Go back to sleep, dear," I said, my voice calmly projecting a false sense of security.

I wish they made a magic pill to cure the problem before me. The only medicines I knew of dulled the senses but wouldn't solve a thing. The decision I needed to make loomed ominously in my mind, like a thunderstorm waiting to unleash its fury. I could only remember having this feeling once before, more than five decades ago, as a child. And now, I felt just as trapped in my own skin as I had then. Then as now, I had found myself staring in a bedroom mirror trying to imagine I was someone else, something else.

One saving grace of my childhood was that I had lived in the country, with acres to roam. Nature became, for me, a place where imagination and reality could coexist without limitation or contradiction. I was a great athlete, a hero pilot, even a wealthy king. I could fade away from difficult reality into another realm where I set the scene to what suited me most. Trees in my world represented stability, offering comfort and shelter. Maybe that's why I was always climbing high into the canopy of any tree that provided a limb low enough to grab onto, and from there I would haul my lithe body up and away. I preferred living the life of a monkey, climbing on trees and swinging from their branches, as they became mountains and buildings. In the world I created, animals were humanlike, plants grew by design, and food was more than just something I ate. Being a monkey freed and protected me from comparison with others and gave me the agility to do things I would never attempt in the real world. My father had a friend who called me Pete. I never knew why. My name sounded nothing like Pete. But in my imagination, it suited me, and I became Pete the monkey. Pete's Fantastic Forest was my kingdom and I its champion. Over the years, my mind effortlessly took the short journey to this place to disguise, dream, and sometimes learn. I even created a journal to track the truths picked up along the way. This magical place was, though I didn't know it yet, preparing me for events lurking just beyond the haze blurring the border between my two worlds. It eventually became a part of who I was destined to be.

The candle's flame moved to the rhythm of our old grandfather clock in a taunting, hypnotic fashion. I felt strangely light. I knew that my mind had been drifting back to the world of Pete the monkey, as it often did. I could pull it back at will, but I enjoyed that world's peaceful calm. The clock's ticking faded, and suddenly I became aware of the smells and sounds of Pete's familiar forest. But a slight gust of wind altered the candle's mesmerizing dance as the bedroom door swung gently open, and in cruel fashion, I was dragged back into the "real" world. "Dang it!" I muttered, then slapped my hand over my mouth. I shifted my gaze to the bed, hoping Ellie wouldn't notice my large frame sitting on her vanity chair. Fortunately, she had fallen back asleep. Libby, our aging Labrador, walked past me. Between Ellie and me, Libby circled once before curling up with her nose tucked under her tail. She let out a soft snort before closing her eyes. Ellie didn't move; she had fallen into a deep slumber. I reached out to pet Libby, but a searing pain caused me to recoil—hot wax from the candle I had just tipped on its side.

Without the candlelight, I could no longer see the mirror. I stood. I would have to do my best to avoid the creaky boards of this old house of ours, but I had become adept at walking that trapeze. I made it safely to the room Libby had just vacated, where the soft cushions of my old lounger was a welcome reprieve for my stiffened back. Fully reclined, I could now see shadows dancing on the ceiling, figures created by exterior lights passing through trees and custom shutters; they mimicked images from my familiar forest. Once again the transcendent forest of my youth beckoned me. I craved its guidance and wisdom.

From a few rooms away, I could hear Libby's heavy sighs. She was quite old for a dog and had been my friend for a good part of my adult life. She knew stories I wouldn't share with anyone else. I imagined her bounding through the shapes on the ceiling, ears flopping and tongue fully extended. And with that image, I found myself fully back in the world of my youthful imagination, the world of Pete the monkey.

I was very young, barely able to walk, as I stretched my youthful hand forward as far as I could reach—and, with welcome relief, seized the vine. With wind whisking through my fur, I was in flight. It was, I knew, a treacherous journey, my inaugural flight into adulthood. I was clumsy and lacked the strength to traverse the treetops alone, but the leaves seemed to pat me on the back, encouraging me to soar. Just ahead was the one I hoped to become. His frame eclipsed the moon's fleeting light on the horizon as he led me through a labyrinth of limbs and branches. I was puzzled at the urgency with which he had encouraged me to attempt this daring leap of faith. Wasn't I still much too young to be learning this? But his reasons would become clear soon enough.

This was my first aerial solo into the forest. It was also the last time I would see my father soaring through the trees on his own. We stopped briefly on a branch, and he began to instruct me in the value of my tail. I would learn that it served many purposes, such as a measure of length and height. But tonight it wrapped around a branch with the strength of a boa constrictor. His voice was calm as always as he explained, "Balance and stability are essential to a fruitful life, son. Remember to always take time to get your balance and survey your environment before you move forward." Recording that thought after returning home was the first time I wrote in my journal—a weathered, leather-bound book of blank parchment. On the upper right corner of the front cover,

Dad had etched his name: *Eugene*. He had given me his own journal to help me to chronicle stories and truths I would learn throughout my life.

 The best reaction is usually no action at all; take the time to understand fully what influences my decision and what is within my control before proceeding.

As I rested and gathered myself, Dad patiently showed me how to maintain balance by holding firmly to the core strength of the tree. I didn't fully appreciate the magnitude of the moment because almost immediately we returned to graceful flight. Our evening ended with his customary smile and his assuring arm resting on my shoulder. I can still hear his voice, full of confidence and encouragement. I should have relished each word. He was not only my dad—he was my hero.

———•◦•———

Those early years were stimulating, filled with promise and innocence. I was fully devoted to the forest. I loved the smell and freedom of the trees. Most mornings, an early voyage lured me: the color radiating through droplets of water resting on leaves, the splashing newness of the day, fluttering wings, a leaping frog, and calming silence. I moved swiftly through the vines, resting only long enough to inhale the majesty of the dawn. This was my routine.

On one such morning voyage, my face pushed through the leaves when I reached the treetop. From here I could see the mountains far to the east—a land in which my dad sometimes traveled, but much too far for a young boy. Still, I longed to go. The south offered trees as far as I could see. I had always heard that a dry, hot, grainy land that would suck you to your death lay beyond the tree line in that direction. I did not know anyone who had actually gone there. The west was dense with both tall and short trees. Some were colorful and others bore fruit. Open spaces where our village friends planted crops sprawled between the wooded areas below me. I lived in a small group of homes we called the Community. Most of our meadows were filled with plants that didn't interest me unless they showed up on our table. My favorite field was the one just below our home. It was the only place in the Community where maize grew. We had tried planting it in other fields, but something about their soil kept the plants from growing. Maize was important to our family. The leaves, when ground into a fine powder and mixed with another substance, made a medicine that kept Mom's lungs from swelling shut. At least that is how I understood it. We grew as much maize as we could in our little field.

As always, I saved looking to the north for last. It was the place I loved to hate. Even from this tall tree, the first thing I saw was that ugly, leafy wall of bramble. It was taller than many of our trees. That was the part I hated. We usually stayed away. You never knew what might jump out of those dark spaces. And really, since nothing else grew near that thicket, there was no need to approach it. To everyone in the Community, it was simply called the Hedge. It served as both protector and prison guard. Most Community residents were happy it kept others out, while some, like me, saw it as the sentry keeping us from our future.

Beyond the Hedge, over the horizon, was the City. Though it was too far to see, I had dreamed of what it looked like. Stories told of those who had escaped through the intimidating Hedge to the freedom of that new world. I never really knew how the stories got back to us because as far as I knew no one had ever returned, but they were powerful truths in our community.

The aroma of fresh bread, as comforting as a warm summer day, pulled me from my observation post. Everyone knew of my mother Raye's baking prowess. She was a fearless master of flour, sugar, and butter, spinning filling and dough into a symphony of flavors. Evenings featured us stuffing our faces with sweet harvest bread as we listened to my parents' stories and I recalled for them every vine and branch that had catapulted me through the canopy. Dad looked at me with pride and smiled. He always laughed at my tall tales. Mom kissed me on the forehead, said "Love you infinity," and sent me to bed. That was our thing, my mom and me—who loved the other one more. *Love you infinity* was the highest. Curiosity enticed me to leave the Community; her love anchored me there. Life was simple.

Our home was modest, unlike those of most of the students in my school. My clothes resembled rags more than riches, and my lunch box was usually light. I had grown accustomed to the growling of an unsatisfied stomach and the art of tactful coughs to cover the embarrassment. My classmates were ruthless, as if calling attention to my shame somehow lifted their status. I was not popular, and my frequent expressions of anger didn't make that any better. I didn't like to be teased, and I always stood up for those less fortunate than even me. That is how the Hedge made me feel. It seemed to separate this forest into halves. I kidded with Herman, my best friend, that the Hedge separated the *haves* and *have nots* (at least based on the rumors we'd heard), but I really wasn't joking. That ominous wall was the gateway to an unknown frontier, but fear kept most of us encumbered.

My friend Herman was different from me. He was taller and much faster. He watched over me as if I were a sapling in the shade of a towering tree. I never felt afraid or alone because Herman was always a vine or two away. Herman and I ran the forest floor, easy and carefree. We worked random jobs in gardens and bundled leaves.

"Come on, kid" he would say. "We can do this together." Our bond was unshakable, forged in circumstance and cemented in love. We were like brothers. We were uncommonly close and somehow able to understand unspoken words, almost clairvoyant.

One hot summer afternoon, that bond was tested. I was a few years younger than Herman, not quite a teenager. He was scrawny, still waiting to grow into his adult body, but much stronger than me. There was a community picnic, complete with food and games. I had just stretched my stomach with an abundance of bananas and cream when Hawk sauntered by. Hawk was my idea of daunting. He was about three times my size and looked twice my age. He was already in high school, so despite my dislike of him, I had to regard him as a champion of adolescence, the battlefield where every teenage male is forced to compete. Underskilled and unprepared, I dreaded that arena. I also lacked the will, or good sense, to say no. Hawk, aware of that weakness, sometimes called me momma's baby boy, which usually humiliated me into a fit of blind rage. On the day of the picnic, I tried to appear busy and confident as he approached. "Hey, Hawk," I squeaked like a baby sparrow.

Hawk leaned toward me and taunted, "How's baby boy today? Think you're man enough to catch some tosses? I have to get ready for the season." His question brought me both the anxiety of challenge with the eeriness of inferiority. *Oh, pizzle.* Even in thought, I used that word rather than the ones Mom and Dad found worthy of soap and an involuntary dental cleaning. We took foul language seriously around our home. That taste was unforgettable.

Hawk was one of our best high school hedgeball toss-ers. Hedgeball required hand-eye coordination, strategy, and courage. The tosser stood about twenty steps away on a fake stump. He threw the hedgeball to a receiver as hard as he could. A striker stood in front of the trencher, a rectangular flat piece of wood, also used to serve food. The position of the thrown ball as it passed over the trencher indicated whether the hedgeball was in or out of the striking zone. The game allowed strikers five tosses to hit the ball. I had tried catching Hawk's tosses before, and he threw so hard it made even the back of my hand hurt as the hedgeball landed in the thinly woven mitt secured by my thumb. But I still agreed; it would have been unthinkable in adolescent male society to refuse the challenge. We wandered far from the festivities, away from the cool protection of the leaves.

"You sure you don't need Mommy to come out and help?" he snarled.

"I'm good," I said with false confidence.

As I squatted behind a makeshift trencher, Hawk didn't throw *to* me, he hurled *at* me with force and fury. It felt as if he was angry at me, but then Hawk always seemed that way. Smack—sting—toss—repeat. The agony became unbearable as mere sting turned to searing pain. I winced each time the ball left his muscular arm and relished the momentary respite as he retrieved my errant throws. He probably knew I did that on purpose.

I gritted my teeth, anticipating the fury of another projectile, when I heard Herman say, "Hey, Hawk, want me to snag a few?" He might as well have said, "Can I save Pete's life?" because that's what I heard. Hawk nodded impatiently, and soon Herman was in the line of fire. That afternoon seemed to last forever as Hawk channeled escalating waves of anger into each throw. I could hear Herman's grunt as pain turned to torture.

Hawk finally bellowed, "I'm going to find one of my teammates. This isn't helping me at all!" Sweet words of relief. I was imagining a perfect throw from me landing in the appropriate part of Hawk's quickly retreating body when I heard Herman throw the mitt to the ground. Herman held his hand to the sky; his third finger had a bend where it should be straight.

That was the commitment we had for each other. Herman took my pain without complaint. I mentally committed that, when I was able, I would return his act of heroic sacrifice. For now, I needed to add a note to my journal.

 Selfless acts of service and compassion are often unnoticed but carry tremendous weight in a relationship.

Chapter Two

In high school, Herman was the successful crushball athlete while I, though I worked hard, spent most of my time on the bench. I did get to see some playing time, but I was never in the spotlight like Herman. Still, I was proud of him. And as for me, what I lacked in skill I made up for in will. I pushed and fought for every second of game time I could get. If it hadn't been for Herman, I don't know how I would have made it through sports, let alone school.

Crushball is a somewhat violent sport requiring physical and mental strength. The term "crush" is descriptive—the basic premise of the game is to advance a ball down a field while the opponents attempt to crush you into the ground. I had the mental acuity but little of the physical prowess required to be successful. I recall one night walking off the crushball field sporting the cleanest jersey on the team and being keenly aware that Dad was not in the stands. That was often true, sadly, but I had learned to accept it. I heard a familiar voice—our neighbor, Mylan. Mylan was a little older than Dad. His son, who was basically good at everything, was a superstar on our team. But tonight

Mylan took the time to seek me out and walk with me for a while. I remember the feel of the grass under my feet as I saw our shadows side-by-side on the field. I didn't recognize what I was feeling at first, but I soon realized it was the warmth of pride, for the first time in a long time. Mylan didn't really talk about crushball. Just about me. He encouraged and complimented me on how I inspired the team. He had been paying attention.

I carried that feeling with me all week.

To my joy, that became a welcome habit. After every game I looked for him and, like the sunrise, he would always be heading my way. Mylan kept up those post-game walks with me until I graduated. He made sure I knew I was important to him. I didn't see it in the moment, but Mylan helped reset the course of my life.

 It is the small, confident voices in my life that build my foundation.

That phase of life was short, and it ended quickly as we graduated and Herman married his high-school sweetheart. I was happy that they were so strong together, but it left me feeling more alone than ever.

Somewhere between my inaugural flight with Dad and leaving high school I discovered what had caused him to accelerate my journey into adulthood. What I hadn't known on that giddy excursion through the treetops was that Dad was sick. Not sick like he ate a bad banana, but sick like he was not going to get better. He first lost his balance and soon after his mobility. Soon he was unable to venture into the forest for his job or for my many school events. Our pantry was becoming bare. My life changed dramatically in a very short period of time. Dad had always been our strong provider. Now he was in our care. As early as high school, I had to learn to shoulder some of that burden for him. Age, I realized, is counted; responsibility is learned. Roles changed as he took my place in the garden and I attempted to fill his shoes in other ways. Looking back, I can only describe his struggle as resolute.

For many seasons, before he became physically unable, Dad had traveled to a village far to the east at the edge of the mountains. His trips were made on a strict schedule. He never missed one. He would be gone for weeks, but he always returned with a small treat for me and a big bag for mom. She seemed relieved and happy to see his return. His routine was the same every time: pat my head, give mom a kiss, hand her the bag, and follow her into the kitchen. I once asked him where he went, and he said he went to a special village where they spoke a different language. The council leader, Marti, was one of Dad's best friends. Dad loved to tell the story of his first visit to that village, where he found Marti standing ominously in the street. "I walked to the edge of the village," Dad would say on each of the many subsequent times he told the story, trying to look very serious as if we did not already know how the meeting unfolded. "And from a distance I saw two large trees in the middle of the town square, near a well. So I approached the well to get some water when one of the trees moved! It was Marti. I was frozen as he barreled toward me." Dad always paused at this point for effect. Then he would stand up on his toes, lean over me, and continue: "His arms were like roots reaching up from the ground enfolding me. Marti then filled the air with a great belly laugh and spouted words that to my ears sounded muddled. Whatever he said must have been positive, because smiling villagers came running from every direction. We talked, we ate, we laughed together, and now we are friends for life." Dad ended that story with a smile every time.

The people in that village were known as the Mahaturens. They had much less in the way of provisions than we did. Their culture was very different from our own. The only similarity he spoke of was a plant growing there that in many ways resembled maize. Over the years, he helped them plant gardens, build habitats, and develop a system to bring water over the mountains to grow more food. Sadly, his illness soon made the journey too difficult for him to travel alone.

One evening Dad had just finished telling me a brand-new story and I had walked into the next room when Mom rushed into the room Dad still sat in. "Eugene, I'm concerned!" She seemed upset. They didn't seem to realize I was still standing in the other room.

"Is it the maize?" Dad's voice was much quieter than usual. Mom explained that the crop was down again for the third season, and her supply of maize would soon be too low for comfort. Dad had built a special storage bin for the fine powdery product harvested from grinding maize leaves. Mom guarded the bin very closely. Sneaking into the kitchen, I lifted the lid and found her concern justified.

"Less than half full!" I said, my voice louder than I had expected.

Then I heard Mom's voice right behind me: "It will be OK." In a comforting tone, she continued, "We will grow more next year." But I could see in her eyes that she was anxious.

Entering the kitchen, Dad said, "Son, it's time for you to travel to Mahaturen. We will go together."

As it turned out, he had been planning this trip for some time. It became an odyssey that would transform my life.

Traveling safely through the forest depended on mobility and on maintaining height above the ground. We needed to move between trees, without descending to the ground, as much as possible. Dad's weakened condition made that impossible for him on his own. But he had designed a harness that wrapped vines and cloth around my waist and over my shoulder, thus securing him to my back. By this time, I had grown large and strong enough to embrace this physical challenge, and within days we were once again in the trees together. I confidently stretched forth my hand and gripped the welcoming vine. The bright sky was a canvas we now painted together with sounds of laughter and smiles of joy. But even that was no match for what I encountered in Mahaturen. Dad's tales came to life, for as soon as our feet hit the ground we were surrounded. I could not release the harness fast enough to allow the sea of arms reaching in to hug my father, and I found myself entangled in the throng alongside him. It was a demonstration of honor, love, and respect; as though they were saying *Welcome, thank you, and goodbye*, all at the same time. The ground in Mahaturen was rockier than the ground in the Community, and the rocks were tinted blue. So rocky was the ground that I couldn't figure out how they grew anything here at all, and yet there were fields of maize-like plants growing everywhere. Series of hollow limbs, unlike any that grew at home, poured water into pools near each garden area. Dad had spoken of this system. The ground almost glowed with blue, an effect apparently caused by the blue rocks.

Dad pulled me aside. "I need to explain some things to you, Son." We sat quietly, looking over the gardens. Marti had retreated to the village as though he knew we needed some time alone. "This place is more than a village I visit from time to time." To my surprise, his expression and his voice were filled with trepidation, as if he were afraid to say what he was about to say. "When I first found Mahaturen, I was on a quest. Your mom's condition had worsened as our supply of maize powder in the Community ran desperately low. Back then, it was your grandfather who supplied the maize powder your mother needed. He would travel to the south and harvest it from a village there. He used it, along with maize, to treat your grandmother and mother both. After he was gone, I took those trips and harvested the seeds to make that powder."

"But wait—are you saying the maize powder is *not* the medicine that keeps Mom's lungs healthy?"

He put his hand on my shoulder and said, "It is both. The maize we grow mixes with that powder and together they make the medicine for your mom."

I was confused, but at least one thing made sense. The bag he always brought to Mom after his journeys was her source of healing.

"When the earth began to dry in the south," he continued, "the plants died and I was no longer able to find it there. I traveled miles in search of a new harvest. It took months. One day I came across this village near the mountains. Marti seemed to know why I was there even without understanding a word I said."

"So the blue earth grows what Mom needs to mix with maize?" I asked.

"It does," he replied. "We call the maize-like plant that grows here Mahatmaize. It is why I come here so often. I work with Marti to sustain these fertile gardens while teaching his village to farm so they can feed their families. They grind the leaves into powder for your mom." I understood the relationship now. They each provided value to the other. They were indeed friends for life.

"Son, you must continue to come here and carry on this work." Dad's expression, along with his voice, had softened.

I already knew what I would say. Watching my dad with Marti when we had first arrived had reminded me of my relationship with Herman. I would be able to easily make new friends here; they already accepted me as Eugene's son. And language would not be much of a barrier. The villagers here had already learned critical words and phrases in our tongue. Mahaturen was now my village too.

I stood and looked Dad in the eye with pride and confidence. As though I was taking an oath, I said, "I will carry this mantle for you, sir."

———————

We stayed in Mahaturen two weeks. That time seemed short. I used it to learn some of their language, and Dad taught me how the watering systems worked. By the end of that time I felt knit into their community, as though we had known each other for a lifetime. Before putting Dad back into the harness, I took a minute to write in my journal.

Purpose reaches to the core of who I am, transcending the barriers of the world and my mind. Committing to my purpose helps me remain true to myself and to see the greater good. A life without purpose is a tree with no limbs.

Mahaturen and the maize had become Dad's purpose in the forest. As we glided through the trees, I heard his voice over my shoulder. The words were like honey slowly dripping in my ears.

"Have faith and follow your heart, Son. Don't lose sight of family, and be true to yourself." This was a lesson in wisdom and truth I would not forget. Watching Dad battle through his physical pain to complete this life-altering task helped me to better understand and honor him. Dad was resolute. I carried more than my dad back from Mahaturen that trip. I added the burden of great responsibility.

"Are you OK?" Mom asked as soon as we arrived. She rushed to Dad, clearly more concerned with Dad and his health than with any bag of powder. I hoped one day to experience their level of love and devotion in a relationship. The odd thought struck me that if I found it, it would probably be somewhere over the Hedge, possibly in the City.

I hurried to the garden to check on our maize. The stalks stood like little warriors. I needed them to hold on until I could find more maize. I crept into the kitchen, and slipped the bin's lid open. I could see almost to the bottom.

"How was the trip?" Mom asked, almost as if to distract me from the nearly empty bin.

I surprised myself with a mature tone: "I have a new perspective now." She smiled modestly, indicating that she knew what I now understood.

In the weeks to follow, I could see how the trip to Mahaturen had taken a toll on Dad's health. His lack of mobility, combined with the pain, now limited him to our home, where he groaned each time he shifted from one hip to the other. Though he could find no comfort, he never complained. When I asked about it, he would just tell me about his faith. That word was as much a part of our family as I was. I tried to have faith in our garden. This season needed to be our best growing season, yet that hope melted when the weather turned fur-shedding hot. When not out searching new areas of the forest, my time was spent in the garden nurturing the remaining plants. I battled daily, wrestling hope from the empty and dark clutches of reality. It was as if an ugly cloud had settled over our lives. The harder I tried, the more desperate things became. Dad would offer words of encouragement, but I knew better. I needed to find new fields of maize, and soon.

Summer was long and hot, but relief eventually arrived. With cooler air came harvest. It provided an adequate bounty to keep the bin at sustainable levels. At least for now.

"That is faith at work, Son." Dad's voice sounded triumphant. "We always have as much as we need, never more than we should have."

I just wanted this fixed. However, I realized what he was teaching me. We cannot change what we do not control, but we can accept it and change ourselves.

Sometimes my best effort cannot force change. Some things are out of my control. The same can apply to people. That does not diminish the value or necessity of trying to bring about positive change.

With the bin adequately filled for a season, I felt the freedom to rest from my diligence in managing the maize supply and seek my fortune. Throughout my childhood, I had dreamed of crossing the Hedge and finding success in the City. I had no idea what the City offered, but I knew it would be amazing. I just knew it. Now that I understood my responsibility to take periodic trips to Mahaturen, I needed to move out of my parent's home, as all young men must. I had stayed home much longer than most of my friends, but Dad's care during his long illness was important. I determined to stay close in order to help him as needed, but far enough away for independence. I would expand my horizons and grow beyond the Hedge.

I tried several random jobs, one after the other, yet nothing seemed to fit. Although work always has a purpose, something was off with each of them. I was at my job cleaning a digestion pit for unused parts of plants when I came to the realization that there must be more to life than this. I had done difficult jobs, hot jobs, even smelly jobs, but the digestion pit was all three rolled into slime. It was awful. Nothing went to waste in our village, and that in itself was great. The not-so-great part was that one of the steps to fully reusing plants was the digestion process. Workers would throw the inedible parts of the plant into a large hole in the ground. The process took a long time and produced an overpowering stench. The best digestion took place in the heat of summer and the final product, a nasty sludgy liquid, was applied to our gardens to help them grow. Standing knee deep in this stink, I thought of Herman. He had always wanted bigger, better, and brighter things, unwilling to believe that what we had was all we could have. To him, the City promised adventure and more. He needed only to make the arduous (or so I imagined) journey past the Hedge, and so he did. I had not heard from him since he and Jo left for the City. I imagined them living in a giant tree, free from worry. I, too, dreamed of life over the thorny barrier that separated me from the mysterious beyond, but I had responsibilities that anchored me in this pit. I could not leave Mom alone. Therefore, I spent the next few months continuing to work odd jobs and spending my free time with my parents and the garden.

Chapter Three

It was fall. The cool breeze ruffled my fur. Mom and I were sitting on a stump having coffee. Dad's condition had worsened, requiring more of my time.

She asked me a puzzling question: "What do you plan to do?" I was trying to think of a clever response when I realized the seriousness of her question. She wasn't asking about tomorrow. She was asking about a lifetime of tomorrows, and offering a gentle nudge to help me out of the pit of indecision in which I found myself. Like years before when I found the courage for my first flight, I had that feeling that my life was about to change. I didn't really have an answer for her. Crickets were now blaring like trumpets. She softly whispered, "Follow your heart to find your purpose." Then, more forcefully, she said, "It is time." *Time for what? Did she know something else that I had not yet figured out?* She stopped me before I could reply. "Son, you are unique. You are not like the other monkeys. Did you ever feel that you weren't living in the same world as everyone else?"

I interrupted with excitement. "Yes! That is exactly how I feel every day! As if I don't fit, or something is missing, or time is moving and I am standing still."

Her smile was reassuring. "Then you are ready." She walked away.

I stared at the bottom of my empty coffee cup. Should I follow her? Just continue to sit in confusion? I chose the latter.

Sometime later, Mom returned to the porch and headed my way. I had never before noticed how gracefully she moved. And the glow on her face reminded me of the bright stars at night. Sometimes I would stare at them for hours, hoping to see one shoot across the sky. But my anticipation at that moment on the porch was even greater.

She carried something in her hands. "What's that?" I asked.

"Be patient," she said. She didn't sit this time. "Our family has a secret that you are now old enough to understand." She had my attention. "Throughout your life, you will be drawn to life's lessons and wisdom in ways that at first may make no sense. When you find a truth, you must record it and commit it to your character. Life's lessons are too valuable to be lost."

I was perplexed. "How will I know what to write? What if I get it wrong?"

Mom revealed the beautiful wooden box she had been holding. It was about the size of the box she stood on to reach the top shelves in our kitchen. The box was dark and secretive, reddish, almost black with deep carvings on every side I could see. It had a lid and one broad peg in the middle of the bottom, carefully chiseled from a different type of wood, so that the box seemed to float a short distance above whatever surface it sat on. The front had carvings of vines intricately woven together, reminding me of the Hedge. On one side there were jagged and pointed images that looked like mountains or even flames. The other side had a magnificent scene with a river flowing through trees and a big meadow. "What's on the back?" I asked.

She turned it around and showed me. "It is blank. This side is for you to carve."

"I don't know how to carve. I don't even have a carving tool." I was puzzled now.

Opening the lid, she pulled out two small objects. One was thick with a flattened end, shaped a bit like my thumb. The other was sharp like the tools we used in the garden, only sharper. She called the second one a sketcher. The first tool she called a tapper. It reminded me of a very small version of the tool we used to drive pincers into our fence.

Before I could even ask, she said, "You will know what to do with them when the time comes." Her voice seemed both encouraging and challenging.

I took a deep breath and leaned back. "We're going to need more coffee," I said, hoping to lighten what had become a very intense moment.

A short time later, we were back on the porch, coffee in hand. "So what else is in the box?" I asked.

"There is one more thing I will show you. Then I must seal the box." She slowly withdrew her hand from the box again and opened it to reveal a shiny string, part of which dangled back into the box. I had never seen anything like this before. It looked almost the same as water reflecting the sparkles of the sun at midday. The string was braided much as one might with fur, leaving no space between each strand. She lifted the string, revealing the prize attached to the end: a round flattened gray object emerged from the box.

"What is that?"

She cradled the object in the palm of her hand. "This is a directional memory piece." She handed it to me. Turning it over, I could see that both sides were slick and etched with small fine lines and dots. It was shaped like a disk, and when I held it, it filled the palm of my hand.

"What does it do?" I asked.

"Nothing," she said with a smile. "The question is what will it help you do." Seeing that I was clueless, she went on. "You will carry this piece with you throughout life's journey. When the time is right, you will know, and the piece will begin to tick and reveal a slender plank from its side or some other guidance. The ticking will be your clue that either you have just learned something worthy of recording on the plank or you must refer to the disk to help you recall something you previously recorded there. Take this sharp tool and etch that principle on the plank and slip it back into the piece. If you are correct, the letters will blaze in blue flame as the disk accepts the plank and the ticking will cease."

My mind was spinning with questions, "How will I know I am finished or what to do next or what the piece is for or—"

Mom's stern voice interrupted. "You will just know; the rest is up to you." Without another word she placed the tapper back in the box and closed the lid. I could hear a loud click as the lid seemed to fold inside the outer walls with no visible way to be reopened. She handed me the disk with the sketcher, now attached to the shiny string. "Keep it with you, always."

———•·•———

I couldn't sleep at all that night. It was as though I walked through a giant spider web. Regardless of how hard I tried, I couldn't shake free from the overwhelming questions stuck in my mind. I pulled at them all night. As soon as the sun lit the horizon, my feet were on the ground. I hurried past the garden and sat on one of the two stumps in front of Mom's home. She finally emerged, two hot cups in hand.

"Well, unique feels better than different," I said. I was eager to get back to the "meat" of our conversation the night before, but thought it best to start slowly.

"How did you sleep?" she asked, her voice cracking a little.

"You know I couldn't sleep!" I cried, and she laughed.

"Then let's get to it." The words I had hoped to hear. "Pause and reflect on your life's journey so far. What important truths have you learned? I'm not speaking of simple truths—I mean the character-building principles that you know make up the fiber of who you will become."

I was eager for that disk to start ticking so I could write something now, but she told me to pause and reflect carefully. Even so, my mind quickly flew through lessons learned from Mom and Dad when I was young. I found affection and value in each story.

"How can I adequately weigh each event? This is a painstaking process," I said.

Mom's voice calmed me. "Each truth you record will reflect a vital value leading you to fulfill your destiny. Be patient and seek ardent moments of truth. What truths truly guide your passion in life?" Her voice fell like gentle rain.

Her question made me immediately think of Dad and of how he was resolute in his pursuit of purpose. And as I thought, I heard a distant ticking. It was coming from my pocket. "Purpose! That must be the first thing I scribe! A tribute to Dad must be first." Pulling out the disk, I could see a small piece protruding from the edge, hardly visible. I tried to pull it free but I couldn't get my fingernail under the edge. I could see a small hole in the center of the protrusion in the tip, but it made no sense.

"Try the sketcher," Mom said with excitement. She seemed as anxious as me. The sketcher didn't offer any obvious options to get under the piece either. I stared at the sketcher's tip and the hole in the center of the piece. They didn't align. Frustrated, I began to toss the sketcher in my hand. I had removed it from the shiny string so it was free. As it turned in the air, I noticed that the flat end was not entirely smooth. I looked more closely and found a small nipple embedded in a recessed area exactly in the center. Placing it over the end of the piece I felt a connection as though they were magnets. With a gentle tug the plank was away from the disk. It was about half the length and width of the sketcher and thin but extremely firm. My hand was shaking; sweat now dripped from my nose. With a deep breath and memories of Dad in Mahaturen, I began to write on the flat surface. ***P…*** The letter sparked into a small blue flame as I wrote…***URPOSE.*** *Purpose* now glowed on the smoky surface of the metal sliver. As I slid it into the disk again, the ticking became louder, followed by instant silence. The edge of the disk was smooth again, exactly as it had been before, with no sign of the plank I had just scribed.

"That was strange." I'm sure the look on my face revealed my surprise, as did the tone of my voice. "I expected something more. What's next?"

But Mom didn't answer, she sat quietly nearby, a tear rolling slowly down her cheek.

I closed my eyes and let my mind wander back to the trees and life before Mahaturen and the garden.

Consequential events rolled by like a parade of light. One strong impression continued to find its way to the top of my mind. "Mylan," I whispered. "He meant so much to me because he always found something positive to say to lift my spirits."

Mom broke my daydream. "What are you thinking, Son? Listen to the disk." It was ticking again, even louder than before. I followed the same steps and etched **ENCOURAGEMENT** on another plank.

Returning the disk to my pocket, I went back to work. *There must be more,* I thought. This was stimulating.

But Mom's voice interrupted my introspection. "Slow down, young man. You need to invest the time to understand and value what you etch into that disk. Purpose and encouragement are very important, but you must allow life to write your story. Don't force it."

But I *wanted* to force it! I was too involved, too energized, to just stop now and wait for life to happen. I'm sure that frustration showed on my face, because Mom quickly continued, "There are important roots to our community tree that you must experience to fully understand. The first has been modeled for you in our family since your birth. We live it every day. You see it in your father's strength and our service to others. When we go down the trail to help our neighbor, or feed the hungry, we are drawing from this root. When your dad is able to sit calmly through pain, he knows everything has a purpose. This root gives him that strength. Faith is that first root. It is faith that gives us the courage to believe in things we can't see. It binds our community together. It is the first and the core root of your life. Strong and impenetrable, it anchors the entire tree with power and stability. When the rains stop, this root draws water from deep within the earth. Your root of faith must reach the depths of wisdom and knowledge to reveal purpose and sustain you through times of drought."

I opened my mouth to speak, but Mom held up her hand to quiet me. I felt as if I were in school again. She continued: "The thumb is the most important digit of our hand. Without it, we cannot grip a vine. It is the unifying member of the hand, and the hand can do little without it. Faith is like the thumb. It is belief in our creator and our purpose on the earth. It guides us by giving us a moral compass. Through faith, I can encourage others to find the good in a situation and grow through adversity, and so can you. It allows us to see opportunity, not fault, while enjoying the journey regardless of the outcome. All this comes through the love in our hearts." She had taken my hand in hers and pressed it against her chest. I could feel our hearts united in rhythm like the ticking of the disk. I wrapped my arms around her neck. Her blanket of love swaddled me. I wanted to etch this feeling on a plank, but there was no need—it was already in my heart.

Tucking the disk away, I headed back to my place. I detoured past the garden and through a familiar part of the woods—where I had taken my first flight with Dad. The disk somehow felt familiar in my pocket. Sitting under that very tree where Dad and I had begun our flight that long-ago day, I closed my eyes. After a few deep breaths, I was relaxed. With rest came clarity.

I put my hand in my pocket and touched the disk. "A directional memory piece," I said aloud, "What does that even mean?" With more questions than answers, I walked the well-worn path back home.

Work was even more challenging in the following weeks. All I could think about was the disk and my future. Crossing the Hedge, saving my mom, and trying to get things moving a little faster. Without a clear plan to follow, I quickly fell back into my old routines. Sleep— work— eat—repeat. Of those three, I liked eating most. Through the warmth of memory, it reminded me of the comfort of the structure of childhood meals at home. Throughout my childhood, the dinner table had been family central, with rules firmly enforced. Wash your face, comb your fur, remove your hat, and always wear a shirt. The odd formality of family dinner was a comforting reminder to appreciate time with family and friends.

I was eager to fill the disk with wisdom, and in my eagerness I became frustrated. The search for wisdom had become a daunting responsibility in the silence of my table for one. I often found myself in deep conversations alone. I needed someone who could understand and help me uncover my purpose to fulfill this destiny of mine. I also felt that it would help to expand the geography of my search—I desperately wanted to get over that hedge and search the fields on the other side. Separating myself from my old life would open new chapters. I needed to break free.

On occasion I treated myself to dinner out in a restaurant surrounded by others. One such evening, I was alone at a corner table as usual and suddenly brightness overcame the night. She was radiant, absolutely breathtaking. I admired her from afar, lacking the courage to say hello. Just watching her chat with friends made me smile. Her laughter was infectious, involving her entire body. Big brown eyes conveyed confidence and compassion in a simple glance. The insecure voice in my head shouted *LOOK AWAY—YOU'RE JUST GOING TO GET HURT*, but she was impossible to ignore and twice as difficult to approach.

I somehow mustered up the courage to stroll in her direction. Surprisingly she spoke first: "I wondered when you would come over." Her eyes smiled as she waited for my reply. My tongue, now inconveniently separated from my brain, could not form a word in response. Trying to help me out, she began again, "Are you here alone? Want to join me?" she continued with patience. I recovered and responded, and our journey began. I knew within minutes that she was my soulmate.

I can't list all the details of how our relationship progressed, but Ellie became my new best friend, the center of my universe, and my wife. She taught me the power of empathy, commitment, and compromise. More importantly, she had faith, and she understood my journey. She permanently filled a second seat at my table while teaching me how to see from a different perspective and how to understand feelings. In every trip with her, I learned to commit, agree on a destination, and compromise. That recipe has served us well. I was drawn to the sincerity of her heart as it revealed the value of benevolence. With Ellie scribed into my heart forever, together we built a home and helped Mom care for Dad. Our time was filled with family and friends. I had horizons to chase, but taking the time to build the foundation of my own family was critical. I came to understand that this delay was an exceptional time of learning and preparation.

We made a habit of taking long walks together in the woods to share our stories and to decompress. Early one morning, on one of those walks, we stopped by a small stream. The brilliant yellow flowers were of a type neither of us had ever seen before. Just above the water's surface floated a pink haze as the moisture evaporated in the dawn. Everything seemed more alive that morning, more than at any other sunrise I could remember. We sat on a log dabbling our feet in the cool water at the stream's edge—as close to water as either of us wanted to get. Smaller animals than us scurried about, making noises of joy and laughter. We found ourselves laughing with them, a connection we hadn't felt before.

"How are we able to do that?" Ellie asked in surprise.

"I'm not sure. It's curious how we seem to understand their feelings," I said. Together, Ellie and I had grown to better understand emotion and feelings. I laughed. "You're always telling me we should try to understand the feelings of those around us. I guess we're both getting better at it."

The sound of my ticking disk interrupted our laughter. It had come to life in my pocket. I pulled the new plank from its edge and quickly wrote *feelings* on it, but there was no blue flame this time. "That must not be the word. What's the word that describes the truth we're experiencing here?" I asked Ellie.

"Silly Pete!" It was what she called me when I was overlooking the obvious, "The word is *empathy*. That's how we understand others." I quickly etched **EMPATHY** on the blank space, relishing the flaming image as I slipped it back into its home.

I needed to remind myself of this so I wouldn't get it wrong again. I made a note in my journal.

 Seeing through the eyes of others opens a new perspective, allowing me to understand and even share in their feelings.

Chapter Four

The next five years were a blur as we grew our family and I cared for Dad, with Ellie and Mom at my side. His endurance surprised me. I was glad he lived long enough to meet my three kids. They were the apple of his eye. He had a name for each of them. Our firstborn was a spring morning. He lovingly nicknamed her Mags because she talked early. She had the gift of gab; rarely a minute went by in silence around her. To him, she was like bright sparkles shining along fresh pathways of adventure, where grass welcomed her curious feet.

"That girl doesn't accept a cloudy day," he would say with pride, watching her speed through a meadow, laughing every step of the way. Her love for life and laughter reminded me of her mother. "Son, encourage her to continue to find the good and to not allow droplets of negativity to weigh her down." That was Dad's way of telling me something without making it about me.

And he was right about Mags. When she was still very young, she sometimes accompanied me to work, and one spring morning she ran into Frank, a grouchy elderly villager who owned a shop next door to where I worked. I had lost sight of Mags for only a minute, and when I tracked her down, I found her in Frank's shop, matching wits with him. His shop door had been left open, and she had marched herself right inside, curious. Much to Frank's chagrin and surprise, this young sprout was giving fullness to his life. Over the next few months, their bond eased decades of his painful memories, and it changed him. Mags frequented his shop. They became two hands of unequal size joined across a vast emptiness, relieving years of pain. Frank didn't have many days left, but he found a new joy as he climbed his final tree with Mags at his side. Her passion for life exceeded even that of my dad and me. The child became teacher to the parent, and I aspired to model her passion for others.

Dad had a unique expression for our second child, Lu, who was a few years younger than her sister. He saw her as the best part of a summer day. "That's my Lu Bug," he would say with pride. He watched her play games as she overcame obstacles and competed with villagers twice her age. The spitting image of her mom, she was naturally athletic. At a very young age, Lu developed a passion for hedgeball. She aspired to be a tosser, a position requiring dedication and work. She would throw for hours, working on one simple skill at a time. Unlike my experience with Hawk, I lived for the moments I could catch her. I welcomed the thump and smack in my mitt.

We found her a tossing coach, Joe, who was as kind as he was brilliant. Much like my Dad, he had lost full use of his arms and legs, only in his case, it was a result of missing a vine and falling from a very large tree next to Herman's old family wheat field. He replaced physicality with patient words and love. I watched as Lu's mental toughness developed through every lesson. She kept Joe as her coach throughout her tossing years. What I remember the most was what Joe would say to her in his calm voice as they ended every session: "One more, Lu, give me one more." Joe taught us both not to limit our skills to physical boundaries. He modeled discipline and faith through every failure and triumph of his life. He always believed in Lu, and she learned to believe in herself through him. His time with Lu taught me the value of dedication and commitment.

Ha, my son, was every season to Dad. The radiance of his smile alone could calm the storm. He had a small chair he would pull next to Dad's and their bond was complete. Ha had a way of looking past physical traits. He never seemed to notice Dad's limited mobility and found ways to spend time with him. Each day he added a little more life to those closing days of Dad's journey.

Ha was the product of two cultures. As our stockpile of maize fell desperately low, I began to travel as far as possible seeking new fields, always finding shelter before the dangers of nightfall could find me. The woods, after all, were dangerous at night for a monkey. The woods to the west were frightful even during the day. Dark creatures roamed freely there—although, fortunately, never near our Community. When I needed to go west, I kept to the safety of the trees.

One particular trip took me south. As when I would travel with Dad, I sometimes traveled for weeks through unfamiliar scenery—but none had been so unfamiliar as the hot, arid south. The trees dwindled away and eventually disappeared. The dirt was gritty and hot to the touch. It slipped under my feet with the heat of burning coals. I fashioned some leaves into mitts for my feet, and for days slogged over the terrain. I quickly learned to avoid the occasional greasy patches along the way. I saw animals sink inexorably out of sight in their inky grasp, disappearing faster the more they struggled to be free. I didn't sleep much, as nightfall brought a chill and I had little to keep me warm. "What an odd place this is," I sighed. I talked to myself just to hear a voice. I welcomed the sight of short bushes and small trees.

My resolute perseverance eventually paid off, and I made it to the village I had set out to find. Unfortunately, what I found was only the remnants of that village.

It looked as if a great storm had broken most of the buildings, leaving the village empty. Beyond the village was water as far as I could see and, along the near shore on either side of the village, mountains too tall for me to climb. Despite all the water, there was no sign of maize or anything resembling the gardens of home. I didn't know where the people of this village had gone, but I feared for them. Then, as I turned to begin my homeward journey, an elderly villager emerged from the debris and approached me. He was holding a bundle of woven leaves. I held my hand up to stop him, thinking he was offering me something for my trip. "I appreciate your generosity," I said, "but I doubt that you can spare anything. Keep it for yourself." Then I noticed something moving within the leaves he held out. It was a naked child. He placed the bundle in my arms. I lost myself for a moment looking in the little one's eyes. He couldn't have been more than a few days old.

"What happened here?" I asked the old villager hoping that he could understand me, but he turned and slipped silently back into the wreckage. "You are a gift, little one," I told the infant with a smile. He smiled back, and I think he smiled the entire journey home. I know I did. Ellie welcomed him as though she believed it was why I had gone on this long journey in the first place. He was so full of joy that Dad gave him the name Ha. He was a friend to every soul he met. I found something much greater than maize on that trip. Ha was the final piece to our family. We were complete.

With the addition of each child, I hoped to hear the ticking of my disk, but silence reminded me I still had much to learn.

———•◦•———

Watching my kids at play was a highlight of my life. They were active in school and church, and they loved our traditional Sunday afternoon meals at my parents' home, a welcome respite at the end of a long week. One Sunday afternoon, as we finished another family meal, Mom asked me about the disk. Clearly, she had something on her mind, and so, coffee mugs in hand, we took a walk to allow for privacy.

"It's true that we are very low on maize, and I know you want to replenish our supply—but your dad is getting much worse," she said in a subdued tone. "You should stop searching for new meadows and spend as much time with him as you can."

My coffee suddenly lost all its flavor, leaving only bitterness in my mouth. I felt waves of unfamiliar pain. Even breath had new meaning. I could almost feel time's methodical pace increasing. His health had always been a risk, but it was surreal to consider that his life could soon end.

Ellie and I spent every possible minute with him over the days that followed. I stopped searching the woods. It seemed futile anyway—maize had become as rare as the ticking of my disk. Life was bearable only with Ellie by my side.

The days seemed like minutes as, with Dad, we laughed, ate, and laughed some more. Dad was still himself. His mind was still sharp, but his body was failing. Even now, though, the strength of his faith remained.

Dad had spent a great deal of his life teaching me about faith. One lesson he introduced using the simplest of acts. Still very young, I had just learned the skill and value of climbing. Being mischievous seemed to be in my blood, so I found myself in precarious situations regularly, but I was usually able to wriggle my way back to safety. One time was different. The limited strength in my skinny arms and legs had been adequate to lift me to a shelf of rock protruding from the side of a steep hill. For a moment I felt untouchable, spying on everyone below and making exciting plans of mayhem. Suddenly the wind blasted my face and then began to swirl around me like a tornado. The reality of height and gravity set in. I could hear roaring in my ears; my hands were sweaty. This wasn't like perching high in a tree, and the foliage nearby offered no security as the crumbling surface of the shelf began to slip beneath my feet. Clutching a thick root I dug free from the rock, I called out for Dad. Fortunately, he wasn't far away. From the ground far below me, he assessed my circumstance and quickly concluded that I must leap into his arms. Was he serious? Jump from this height? I tried to negotiate a different escape route—couldn't he climb up and rescue me? I was stuck and afraid.

I recall the words he spoke next, and the tone of his voice, as if it were yesterday. In a voice as calming as a sunset, he said, "Pete, have faith. You must trust me." But I didn't let go of that root yet. He had to keep trying. Eventually, though, he convinced me to let go, trust his strength, and make that terrifying leap. And just like that, I was resting safely in his arms.

"Faith," he told me as he carried me back toward home, "is believing in something so much that you forget your doubts and fears. That is trusting. Once you trust something or someone, you will be able to let go of your fears and hold onto their strength." And that kind of faith was what I saw in him as he faced his final climb. He had faith in his creator and was ready to let go and leap into those strong arms. We grasped every moment tightly. He worked hard to just be himself, the Dad I knew, right to the end. His final days were an outpouring of knowledge and experience. He spun stories like spider silk. Those final quiet times offered reflection and clarity. Some memories, leadership truths to remember, found their rightful place in my journal.

One favorite memory was of a time the two of us spent in his workshop before his illness exiled him to the confines of a chair. We built nothing significant during that time, but wisdom streamed from his mind. That afternoon we were exploring the concept of continuous motion. Dad believed a wheel could be made to turn without stopping. He was meticulously placing magnets at the end of rods as thick and round as my finger and half the length of my arm, connected like spokes in a wheel.

"Magnets exert a force that attracts or repels other magnets," Dad said as he worked. These magnetic fields, he explained, somehow created motion. He believed that magnets continually drawn to the attracting field of a flanking magnet on the wheel would create unending motion. Of course, to succeed, he would have to defy the effects of friction and gravity. Friction won, but Dad always believed he was one test away from the answer.

He pulled a handful of magnets from the jar and aligned them on the workbench. Each was exactly the same. Their shape reminded me of the imprint left in the dirt when wild horses came through. As he moved them across the bench, some magnets darted away while others quickly connected to the one in his hand.

He looked up and said, "This is a model of strong leadership. Apply this concept and you will influence others in a powerful way." I nodded, only half paying attention—I mainly just thought the magnets were cool. "Villagers have different skills and traits," he went on. "They also, like these magnets, have unique charges, both positive and negative. Magnetic leadership requires that you first understand your own magnet before you engage others. Leading is connection, and connection requires a deeper relationship with those you lead. Present an inviting magnetic face, and others will join your vision. That requires discipline and self-awareness." Dad's lessons often went over my head, but this time, I began to understand what he was saying.

Seeing that he had piqued my interest, he pulled a sheet of paper from the dark oak cabinet that held his nails, screws, and washers. "Son, pay attention. We all have behavioral tendencies—what you might call our magnetic fields. They are charged not with electrons but with emotion. Magnetic leaders will recognize and manage their feelings as they pivot their face toward others. This enables them to attract supporting forces and repel detractors. Facing the same direction as similarly charged supporters creates alignment but not connection. Forcing head-to-head engagement, on the other hand, repels and creates disruption, and that disruption is usually expressed with passion. Effective engagement attaches strength to a need. I will give you some examples to help you understand. Use this model to develop continuous motion in your leadership." I realized that he was encouraging *me* to become a leader, and I felt a deep sense of pride.

"The hallmarks of this leadership style," he continued, "are self-awareness and dynamic change. Life change is always accompanied by emotion. Here's a handy and effective way to evaluate the power of emotion in yourself and others." With a carpenter's pencil, he began to write on the sheet of paper.

MAGNETIC LEADERSHIP
Use this checklist to identify your current emotional charge and to fill in the model below. Check only one behavioral tendency in each category.

1. When you are happy, would you rather:
   ☐ Celebrate with others and enjoy laughter (outward)
   ☐ Reflect on life and quietly relish the time (inward)

2. When you are unhappy, would you rather:
   ☐ Visibly express your feelings with nonverbal cues (outward)

❑ Recede into your thoughts, saying very little (inward)

3. When you have a firm belief that something is right, do you:
❑ Express your view with passion and confidence (outward)
❑ Quietly let your actions speak, modeling conviction (inward)

4. When you have a strong belief that something is wrong, do you:
❑ Become argumentative and forceful (outward)
❑ Hold quietly to your beliefs (inward)

5. When you are giving or receiving positive news, would you rather:
❑ Have a face-to-face conversation, physically relating emotions (outward)
❑ Have indirect contact, allowing the news to be received in private (inward)

6. When you are giving or receiving negative news, would you rather:
❑ Have a face-to-face conversation, physically relating emotions (outward)
❑ Have indirect contact, allowing the news to be received in private (inward)

7. What refuels you the most? Select only one:
   - ☐ Conversation (outward)
   - ☐ Recognition (outward)
   - ☐ Serving (inward)
   - ☐ Reflection (inward)

8. When you first engage a new group, would you rather:
   - ☐ Mingle and introduce yourself (outward)
   - ☐ Sit and allow others to come to you (inward)

Write your preferences along the magnet below.

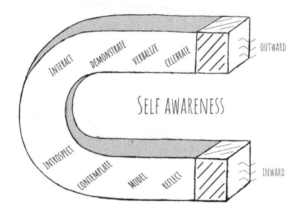

This magnet demonstrates how you express yourself in four critical leadership charges.
I. Ethics—Right/Wrong
II. Communications—Positive/Negative

III. Feelings—Happy/Unhappy
IV. Connection—Refuel/Engage

Effective leading pivots your magnetic engagement charge to connect, align with, or reject others. Misaligned magnets create tension and anxiety. The choice is not whether to interface—it is the face with which we enter.

I remember observing these attributes with the Mahaturens as Dad overcame cultural and language barriers. His life connected a series of magnets within and beyond our community.

 As a leader, I will align all attributes while reducing friction within my team.

Chapter Five

The wind was colder that day and the sun a little less brilliant. I was wearing a dark suit that smelled a little funny. I wore it only for formal occasions and really didn't like it much. Now, my grip on the handle was failing me as I struggled to carry him one last time. It wasn't so much the weight as it was the finality of the moment. I could almost feel his arm on my shoulder again, could almost hear his voice say, "Perk up! Put a skip in that step." Tears were flowing uncontrollably down my cheeks. I had tried to prepare myself for this day, but it hadn't really helped. Through my swollen eyes, I saw Mom and Ellie standing at the edge of his open grave. I wanted to appear strong for them, but I was carrying much more than my hero that day. He had invested so much in me. He had uncovered strengths I never thought possible.

Adding to my anguish was the knowledge that our maize supply was desperately low. I could not lose Mom too.

When the time came to say my final goodbye, I picked up a plaque from the ground. My hands were shaking so badly that I almost dropped it before I managed to place it just below the flowers. It read, "Eugene, Beloved Husband, Father, and Friend—*Resolute in Pursuit of His Purpose.*" The forest had a different sound now, almost reverent. I looked back at his marker. Those words were all I had left to give, a reminder how obstacles become stepping stones when we are resolute in pursuit of our purpose, as my dad had always been.

As we walked back down the path, I could hear the muffled ticking of my disk. A little sideways grin broke across my face as I realized, *Of course, Dad would want me to record it here. Even in death, he is teaching me.* I stopped and etched **RESOLUTE** on the plank and quickly slipped it back into the welcoming disk.

Mom, Ellie, and the kids had moved ahead of me down the path, leaving me to my thoughts. I reached for my journal to make a brief entry to commemorate the life of my hero.

 I lost my father, mentor, and my first friend today. His life taught me many things, but one profound lesson: If I believe in my purpose, I must be unwavering in my commitment to pursue it.

I hurried to catch up. Mom hummed some familiar songs that reminded us of him. I admired her. Being a lifelong caregiver had not been in her plan so many years ago; yet, she had never complained or faltered.

The next few weeks were difficult. Packing up his personal belongings and removing the apparatus that aided in managing his life uncovered painful memories. I had been fortunate to help care for Dad, but I had no doubt whose service had been primary. Mom anchored our family. It amazed me how little she required. We were the weathered limbs under a heavy load that she held as her life bent, but did not break.

And now that Dad was gone, she continued to invest in me. Once again, Mom and I found ourselves staring at our dark reflections in the coffee we loved so much. Mom was sitting in her rocker; I settled onto a stool nearby. There were softer and more comfortable places we could sit, but this was familiar. It was us. It was not a warm day, and it felt damp. The dim sunlight offered little relief. But then Mom suddenly changed the mood, pivoting to memories of Dad. I loved reminiscing about his affection for Ellie and the kids. For hours, Mom shared stories that made us both laugh. Then she fell eerily silent. Her serious expression indicated that something solemn was coming.

"Son, there is a second root to our community tree that reaches out much farther than the deep root, searching beyond the shade. This root runs not deep but far and retrieves nutrients we do not have in our home soil. Sharing outside experiences brings strength to community life. I now need you to find it beyond our boundaries."

"What do I need to do?" I asked, dreading what she would say next.

She looked almost desperate, "I am rationing maize now. We are almost out. Though I nurture the remaining plants, their harvest produces less each season."

I was shocked but not surprised. I had been watching the fields. "I need to go beyond the Hedge to find more maize," I said. At last, I had found the courage to face that fear and cross the Hedge, rather than simply talking about it.

Softening her voice, she leaned into me and whispered, "It is more serious than you know." Mom paused a long time, then said the last thing I would have expected her to say, something I would have heard only in my worst nightmares. "Your children have the potential of being sick, like me. They just haven't displayed symptoms yet, but they could. You see, my illness is hereditary. It has been a part of our family for generations."

"Which child?" I asked, my skin quickly turning cold.

"The gene passes only to females born into our family. Both of your daughters may have it. We won't know for sure until they are older." Her face showed deep sadness. I suddenly felt dead inside, as if all the joy had been sucked out of me. I dreaded telling Ellie. This would break her heart. According to Dad, the role of a leader takes on many forms. I did not want this one.

Mom stuck her index finger out, "Think of family as this finger on your hand. It is stronger when supported by faith. For this finger to stand alone requires the thumb to hold the other fingers in their place as a foundation. In the same way, you will need your family to help carry you through this quest."

She had given me a waterfall of responsibility, and I felt as though I had only a small cup with which to catch it. I poured out my cold coffee and Mom and I embraced. I longed for my disk to tick, because I wanted to etch *family* on one of its planks. But no need. It was already etched on my heart.

"We do this together!" Ellie's voice filled with passion. "I want to be absolutely clear about this—if we're leaving here to find a supply of maize, then we'll do it as a team." I had already explained the frightening and challenging details of our genetic enemy. Now, knowing that this unseen threat was a danger to her own children, her determination didn't waver. I was comforted by the strength I saw on her face. It reminded me of Dad.

Ellie went right into planning mode. "We need to take the kids with us. I won't allow our family to be torn apart through this. Whatever happens, it will be all of us in it together." Those big brown eyes were slightly larger now, with the intensity of an owl in the night.

Everything moved quickly. The kids thought we were going on a long family adventure, and like me they were excited to see what was beyond the Hedge. We didn't discuss the risks in detail with them; we thought they were better off not knowing. "Pack only what we can carry," she said. Ellie was in full command now. Family adventures were her territory. Within days, we were ready to face whatever we would have to face. Stepping away from our home, we made the short trek to the Hedge. Now, knowing that we were about to push our way through it, It seemed as threatening as though it were a malevolent, living thing.

"Herman and Jo made it through somehow," I said, trying to instill confidence, but Ellie knew we hadn't heard from them since the day they left. No one, in fact, had ever returned from beyond the Hedge. I found it ironic now how, as I was growing up, I believed the Hedge provided protection, keeping predators out. By the time I was older, I had grown to think of it as a barrier, keeping me in. Today, it was the obstacle standing between us and salvation. Failure was not an option.

Stopping at the edge of the bare, infertile ground that skirted the Hedge, almost as if it the Hedge drained all of the water for some distance so that nothing else could grow, we sat for one final rest. To lighten the atmosphere, I grabbed my bandolin—an instrument with a long neck and thin, sharp strings. I loved playing it, and sometimes sat for hours and serenaded any passerby who would listen. When learning a new chord, I sometimes had to stretch my fingers to their limit. Now, moving beyond the Hedge was stretching us. But change, as dangerous and scary as it sometimes is, is necessary for growth. I pulled the journal from my bag. The worn leather gave me comfort. The faded letters spelling *Eugene* gave me courage. I took time to write on the wrinkled pages.

 Flexibility requires time, patience, and perseverance. If I do only what I have always done, I can't grow as life changes around me. Moving beyond my comfort level opens a world of possibility.

I packed my journal, shouldered my pack, and walked to the Hedge, closer than I ever had before. It was more intimidating than I had imagined. In fact, it seemed impenetrable. I couldn't see through it. If I stacked all four of my family members on my shoulders, they still wouldn't be able to reach the top. It ran as far in either direction as I could see. There was no way over or around it. The only way forward was straight through. I had no plan for that—I just bent my knees and tried to push through the outer layer to test the thickness. I was able to push my head and shoulders through that layer, and once past, I could see faint glimmers of light. As I pushed further, the Hedge tore at my skin with a barrage of barbed tines. Sharp pangs fired through my body, and I pulled back. "I can see the other side!" I shouted to the family, trying to sound more optimistic than I was. The last thing they needed was a reason to give up. I tried to push through a few more times, but finally had to step away and stop to rest. Trickles of blood and sweat dripped from my arms, face, and head. I must have been a horrifying sight. In fact, Ellie turned the kids away and moved them back a little further from me. After I'd cleaned off the mud and debris, though, I wasn't as intimidating. The shallow scratches didn't continue bleeding, but they still stung. Presentable now, I rejoined the family circle. Their calm faces were reassuring.

"We have a plan," Ellie said. "The kids and I have been watching you press into those spikes. The bottom of the hedge pushed upward each time, revealing a path beneath. We can crawl under."

I was embarrassed—shouldn't I have been the champion that defeated this beast? Instead, I'd spent an hour forcing attempts at the same failed solution while they solved the puzzle. I always expected so much of myself. Overcoming personal failure and disappointment was hard for me, but this had illustrated for me an important lesson. Working alone, I felt small. Together, we were bigger than the Hedge.

 I learned the value of teamwork today. While I was busy confronting an obstacle, my family (the team) working together, were able to overcome it. I must remember to include others in the process.

Wrapping my arms and head in tough, leathery leaves, I again knelt in front of the Hedge's jagged limbs. I leaned into it as far as I could, just as before, and then I lifted upward with all my might. I could feel my family, prostrate in the dirt, crawling past me under the Hedge.

"There are no thorns in here," Ellie called.

When they were all in, I eased away from the Hedge. Ellie had placed a large piece of bark over her back, and left one for me as well. Now she pressed upward on the Hedge from beneath as I lay on my belly and crawled under. Slipping past her, I was again with my family.

"This is fun, Dada!" Mags's voice echoed in the mysterious cavity. There was space for all of us. But, unsure what else might be sheltering in the well-protected opening beneath the Hedge, I decided not to linger. It was much easier to press our way out than it was getting in. We used the protective bark to mark our spot. "Now we have a safe way back to Grandma," Lu said with a smile. She was right; we had found a passageway through the previously impregnable fortress.

The trees on this side were similar to the ones at home. I saw nothing else—just woods as far as I could see. "Let's explore ahead," I said, shouldering my pack.

We walked for most of the day before I began to notice changes. Trees became gradually fatter; their dense bark reminded me of the scaly skin of animals I'd seen in the creamy hot land far to the south. The trees' limbs were becoming sparse, and none of them grew close to the ground. And beneath the trees we found only bare dirt. We dropped to our knees and dug—the dirt was like powder with almost no moisture. I had been hoping that, by the time we needed to find a place to sleep, we would find somewhere similar to home, but this area was so much drier and felt unfriendly.

"Nothing but trees will ever grow here." Ellie sounded dejected.

I spoke with all the faith I could muster: "Let's keep searching. We'll find something."

As we moved on, I kept the sun on our left side to be sure we weren't walking in circles.

After what seemed like many hours, I heard Mags cry out, "It's a field, Dada." She had run ahead, as usual, and now raced back leaping and shouting as loud as she could. Over her shoulder, I could see brighter sunlight as the woods opened to a clearing.

"What a relief," Ellie sighed. The wind's continuous motion caused the leaves and grass ahead to roll side to side, with waves of color stirring in the breeze. I could hear the call of a bird circling overhead. That was new—the birds at home sang only at night, stopping suddenly at any sign of danger. This song was happy, as if it were calling us home. And yet this wasn't really home, and the melodies of birdsong and wind were new, not the familiar sounds of our forest.

We slowly moved toward the sway of the landscape. There was extremely tall grass stretching across an open meadow.

"I wish it was maize," Ellie said as we stepped out of the darkness of the forest. The grass had bright green stems and, at the top, dark yellow flowers holding white balls. It was a symphony of motion in an expanse of color, and we felt overwhelmed, in awe. I stretched out my hand to touch a ball, but it puffed out of reach, drifting like powder. The meadow spilled onto rolling hills in the distance, and on the far side stood a darker rim that appeared to be a wall of leaves only slightly taller than me—not trees, but much taller than grass. A long-eared fur ball bounced up from the grass nearby and raced away from us as fast as it could go—which was very fast. The kids bounded through the tall grass, picking flowers and spinning tumbles into giggles. The tall green stems became their playground.

Ellie and I sat in a clearing for a long while and basked in the sunlight. Far ahead, I spied something that looked like indistinguishable humps of some sort. Boulders? I started to comment on them but Ellie broke the silence first. "Where do we go from here?"

Though I had no idea, I said, with false bravado, "Let's move toward those odd mounds in the distance." Orange flowers growing between the patches of tall grass suddenly distracted her, and she busied herself weaving a bracelet. It seemed like a good distraction for the moment.

I stood and stretched, thinking we should continue on soon, when a movement caught my attention. "Did you see that?" I asked Ellie, trying to sound casual as I pointed toward where I'd seen the movement, near the mounds. Our eyes had not yet fully adjusted to the brightness after the shade of the forest. But as I squinted into the distance, it became apparent that we were not alone. Something was scurrying on top of the mounds. I could now see the mounds themselves better. They had oddly tall limbs rising from their center. Some were puffing dark smoke into the sky. More moving images came into sight, moving randomly between hills and space. A small group of creatures was intentionally moving in our direction. They didn't look exactly like us—or like each other, for that matter. Some were thin, others were bulky, but most of them seemed short like Ellie. The very slow ones had bowls on their backs. I recognized the furry one with the long ears—it was the same type that had bounded up near us and raced away.

Making contact was inevitable now, and although the idea seemed intimidating, this was what we had come for. I sent Ellie and the kids back to the edge of the trees. The forest might provide a quick exit should things not go as I hoped. We were, after all, monkeys—we could climb trees if we needed to. With a firm upper lip and shaky knees, I walked to meet them. I could hear their voices before their faces came fully into view. I recognized their words—they said something about *friendly* and *danger*, but their tone seemed welcoming.

But as soon as they were close enough, they called out, "Hello, how are you? Where are you from?" That was all I needed to hear. I could see their smiles now, accompanied by waves and welcoming gestures.

I had not heard Ellie approach behind me, but suddenly her voice was at my shoulder: "Let's go," she said softly as if she were telling a secret. She walked past me toward the welcoming delegation, and the kids followed her, leaving me to bring up the rear.

Chapter Six

Two friendly characters, roughly our age, were the first to greet us. "Welcome to the Town. My name is Jay. This is my wife Emma. Where y'all from?" They talked a little funny, but I kind of liked it. There was a warmth about this group that seemed almost organic. A group of slender, delicate animals approached, joining some burly, well-fed companions; they all shared some laughter as they ambled down the path. One after the other—small, short, heavy, thick, furry or not—animals moved along the path and between the mounds as close as a family.

"Hi, Jay, I'm Pete, this is Ellie. I see your daughters have already met my kids." It was refreshing to see our three playing with other animals again. "Can you tell me about these mounds of dirt?"

"They're our homes," Emma said with a smile. "We dig them about as deep as they are tall, so essentially we live under the ground. We call them berms."

"What are those poles sticking out of the top?" Ellie asked.

"Smokestacks. Berms are cool all year. We build fires inside to cook and keep warm." She had started walking back down the trail toward their village, and we followed, along with the rest of the group. Her expression became more serious. "We never, ever go out at night. Berms are shelter from—" she stopped herself mid-sentence and then continued—"Well, they keep us safe at night. Come on, Jay and I will take you to our home."

They lived on the east edge of the Town. Emma took Ellie inside the berm to show her how the smokestack worked. Jay and I stayed outside to see his garden, surrounded by a large field on three sides. Jay proudly explained how they grew every kind of root vegetable. The soil was very dark and loose, a perfect medium for growing the sort of plants whose roots they dug up and ate. "Plants whose edible parts grow above the ground, like fruit or greens, don't do so good here," Jay said.

"Have you ever grown maize here?"

"Nah, I ain't sure I even know what maize is." Watching Jay's face for any sign of recognition, I described the plant and how we used it.

"Yep—now that sounds like sweet flower." Jay was smiling as if he had just won a game. "We don't grow that in our garden though. I think there's an empty berm, on the west side, that has a few sweet flower plants. The dirt over there is tougher than ours. You should see about settling in over there. It needs some fixin' up, but you can become dwellers like us."

I was too excited to ask what he meant by *dwellers*. I looked around to see if Ellie had heard us. She and Emma climbed out of the berm, chattering and carrying on like sisters. Ellie had missed this, I knew. Mags, Lu, and Ha were roaming the fields with Jay and Emma's daughters. Already this began to feel like home—at least for now. After a quick tour of their property, we all walked back to the Town. Emma met with the Town leadership to explain about us while we walked around their shops. Ellie stopped to watch an artist sitting outside on a stool expressing life in color. She signed her work *Loraine the Dweller*. I learned that *dweller* is what they called community members who lived there. Loraine was creating beautiful pictures on flat pieces of bark; later, we would learn how carefully she stripped the bark from a grove of trees that grew by a little stream, then cleaned, shaped, and pressed them flat. Her pictures were landscapes of the scenery we had passed on our way from Jay and Emma's berm. Ellie bought a few, since they would look nice in a new home.

"You can move in!" Emma called, beaming, as she approached us. She had convinced the Town leadership to allow us to move into the abandoned berm Jay had described.

Jay and Emma pointed us in the right direction and then headed home. Our family hurried down the trail. It would be dark soon, and we remembered what Emma had said about going outside after dark. The berm that was to be our new home felt familiar somehow, maybe because of its proximity to the woods. The fading beams of sunlight fell across a small garden—and yes, it contained stalks of maize. I smiled at those new soldiers as though they had been awaiting our arrival.

Inside the berm, the stench of wet sod was not the best welcome, but Ellie was our litmus test—if she was happy, I was happy. I kept one eye on her as the other scanned crevices for unwelcome guests. Ellie finally closed the door and with a simple nod, she went to work making it look more like home and less like compost.

Turning to the kids, she gave the verdict, "We are now dwellers." We were also safely through the Hedge.

 I often fear what I don't understand, viewing it only through my lens. Objectivity is seeing through different lenses to gain perspective.

That first night was intense. My family had never slept outside the Community. Somewhere between rest and sleep, I heard a cry—loud enough to rouse me, but not so loud as to cause alarm. Maneuvering the foreign space, I made it to the front door. I heard it again, coming from the meadow. Curiosity took me as far as the garden, where caution brought me to a stop. The agonizing sound seemed much closer now, almost right in front of me. More like a screech than a scream, it moved—like a voice echoing in a cave. As if it came from everywhere. Gathering my courage, I moved past the garden, then froze again as caution became fear.

The first shadow passed so quickly I couldn't make it out, couldn't even conclude for sure that something had rushed past me until it was long past. But the smell lingered, removing all doubt. In the dim moonlight, it had looked dark, almost like rolling smoke. Just as the rank odor began to dissipate, the shadowy figure came into sight again, only from a different direction. *Could there be two?*

I began walking slowly toward the door when another shape emerged from the berm's shadow. It was hard to make out in the dark—I had a sense only of its lowered head and hunched shoulders, its mangy pelage, and its snarling teeth, all of which suggested that it was not friendly. I felt the blood drain from my face as I heard deep breathing behind me.

KABOOM!

The sudden explosion startled me so much that I fell. When I struggled to my feet and looked wildly about, I realized that my pursuers were gone.

"You all right?" It was Jay. "I figured they'd get you to come out. They're always watching. They prey on the mistakes of inexperienced dwellers. Once you're circled—" he shook his head—"you're toast!" The crude wooden box in his right hand had a rope swinging by its side, entering the box through a hole. The big stick in his other hand ended in a sharp piece of metal that told me Jay meant business. It was like a really long knife from the kitchen.

"Was that an animal?" I said, staggering to my feet, still shaky.

"We call them shadow beasts." Jay's voice was calmer now. "They've lurked in the dark as long as I can remember."

"Will they hurt you?" I said, hoping to calm myself.

"They'll kill you if you give 'em a chance," Jay said. "We've lost entire families to the shadow beasts. If they get you alone there isn't much you can do. My fault—I should have explained all this this afternoon."

Why had I not seen the shadow beasts before, or even heard of them? I had heard that some manner of dangerous beasts lived in the west, but whatever they were, they never came around our community.

I was thinking more clearly now. "What was that sound?"

"I call this my beast box," Jay said, patting its side. "Dwellers have used 'em against the beasts since before I was born. The booming sound scares 'em away." The box held a flat piece of metal secured to a rope. Pulling and quickly releasing the rope made the sound. "Stay in your berm at night if you want to survive," Jay continued, "no matter what you hear. These things are clever."

"Have you ever seen one up close? Do they all smell that bad?"

Jay turned toward home. "Most times, when you see one, you don't live to talk about it. Just stay inside at night." His voice was friendly but firm. A cold feeling came over me, and then a realization: *Maybe the Hedge was there to protect our community from dangers such as this.*

The next day, I evaluated the health and maturity of each maize plant. There weren't many, but they were strong. This would sustain Mom while I searched for more. Things seemed to be falling into place.

Ellie's help would be crucial; I would not be able to do this without her. Even as a leader, I needed an accountability partner and anchor. She was that and more, my calming voice in a storm. I once saw a family of deer run into a mire and bog down there, unable at first to free themselves. The more they struggled, the deeper they sank. The buck, with massive strength, burst free momentarily, only to fall back again and settle deeper into the quagmire. Two fawns cried, sunk to their bellies and too young and weak to free themselves. But the doe, sunk in the mire like the rest of her family, remained unusually calm. Almost motionless, she bleated gentle support to her family while calmly, with slow, steady, gentle movements, freeing herself. A short time later, all four were resting safely on solid ground and shaking themselves clean. The doe's calm and her gentle example had become their strength. That was Ellie.

Over time, Jay and Emma taught us about gardening in this soil, growing our friendship along with our crops. When harvest approached, I grew excited to take some home to Mom. Our new friends' eagerness to share skills and knowledge had helped us survive and flourish.

It is important to listen to those who have been where I am going to learn from their experience. I don't have to know everything. I just need to listen to those who know more than I do.

When our first harvest was complete, it was time for the journey back to Mom and the Community with a supply of life-giving maize. Leaving early in the morning, I moved quickly, allowing plenty of time to make it safely through the Hedge before dark. I was pleased that it offered little resistance to the shield of wood I'd prepared.

My attitude changed quickly when I reached Mom's house and saw her garden bare, without any hint that it had even been planted or cared for this year.

"Mom!" I shouted, fearing the worst. Her home, when I rushed in, looked uninhabited, with dust and webs everywhere. It felt as if no one had been living there for weeks. I burst into the kitchen—her favorite spot—in a panic. My spine froze at the sight of the cluttered counters in a dark room. Then:

"Pete, is that you?" came her weak voice. Greatly relieved but still concerned, I rushed into her bedroom. My heart sank. The room was uncharacteristically messy. She was in bed in late afternoon. I couldn't recall ever seeing her like this before. .

"Are you sick?" I already knew the answer.

"I'm just tired." The words didn't mask the obvious—just sitting up seemed to exhaust her. Then she saw my bag of maize, and new energy appeared to surge through her. Holding my arm, she was able to walk into the kitchen. My harvest provided enough powder to fill half the storage bin.

"That will last me for months," she said with a smile.

"I'll grow more next season." I felt calmer now. "There are large meadows near our home, and I'm searching for sites for larger crops."

I stayed a few days. With the powder I provided, her health restored quickly. She assured me that she would reach out to the Community for help if she felt ill again.

———•·•———

Now that our maize was healthy and growing, I needed to find work and then search for maize as time allowed. Jay told me of a nearby factory where many dwellers worked. A short walk later, I found a group of large white structures in a grove of trees. Small furry striped animals, with short tails, raced back and forth focusing their efforts on gathering nuts—dark with yellow spots—and depositing them in wagons. Some of the nuts were still hanging in trees; others had already fallen to the ground. These little animals were all humming the same happy tune, which appeared to keep them all working at the same pace.

I tried to stop one, but he politely chided, "Sorry—let me get back to work."

Their dance of purpose was eventually interrupted by the sound of a horn, which sent them to the shade for rest, sitting in small groups.

I approached another worker. "Excuse me."

"Hey, what's your name?" the young worker replied.

"I'm Pete. What's yours?"

"My friends call me Spots," he said, pointing to an odd grouping of spots on his shoulder.

"What do you do here?"

"We are gatherers," he said, standing up on his four little legs. "We gather nuts for the City Nut Company, or CNC. We've been doing this for generations."

"The *City* Nut Company?" I said. "You know where the City is?"

"Nope," he shouted, and scurried back to pick more nuts even before the horn sounded again. It was obvious that he and his co-workers took great pride in their work. I later learned they collected nuts to help feed all the citizens in the City. That was their purpose. I wondered how they could spend their entire life doing the same thing, day after day. I jogged beside another busy worker and asked about the tune they hummed. He didn't stop, but as he scrambled away he pointed toward the factory.

"It's the song of JB, our general manager." I could barely hear his voice as he shouted back over his shoulder. "Ask him!"

I tracked JB down—not in his office, but at the edge of the field, overseeing the work. He was larger than me, sporting red fur and an encouraging smile. He reminded me of Mylan. He spoke devotedly about CNC—its history, its products, its customers. I could feel his commitment.

I asked about the song. He continued to smile, but his eyes issued a challenge. "You have to work here before you can understand. Nut gathering is important work."

The next morning I was back before dawn to accept his challenge, embracing my new job with exuberance. Much larger than the other gatherers, I proudly grabbed a bag and walked into the grove. A bounty of nuts lay under every tree. Quickly dropping my first prize in the bag, I looked down, spotted another, and reached for it. A rush of fur and fiber preceded my reach. Workers had surrounded me before I could bend over again. The ground was clean. They were quick little critters. Picking up my pace, I found random nuts along the way, but my bag was filling slowly. A horn finally sounded, calling us to a short rest and suspending my frustration. My half-full bag hit the ground next to my body as I plopped in the shade next to an elderly gatherer.

"How did you do?" he asked, his eyes teasing.

"It was harder than I expected, but I filled half my bag," I said apprehensively. "I think you need to call me a gleaner instead of a gatherer."

"Nut picking is gatherer's work," he said, grinning now.

"How did you do?" I asked.

He smiled for a minute, calmly nibbling his snack. "Just emptied my sixth bag."

"Six bags!" I hadn't meant to say it so loudly, but I was shocked. I felt pathetic. Then that wretched horn sounded again, sending us back to the trees.

Mercifully, the day came to an end, along with my energy. I had heaved only five full bags into the wagon all day. Humbled, I could hardly move as I walked home that day, surrounded by the tiny gatherers. And it didn't get better with time. After two weeks, I could fill barely ten bags a day, merely half the average gatherer's work.

Not surprisingly, there was a note in my locker the first day of my third week.

PETE.
PLEASE SEE ME AT THE END OF YOUR SHIFT. LEAVE YOUR BAG IN YOUR LOCKER.
JB

That day seemed especially hot. I was distracted and nervous. JB was standing in a field when I finished my shift, where he normally was.

He shook my hand and said, "Pete, I applaud your effort. How do you feel?"

"Embarrassed and frustrated," I said.

He nodded. "I'm glad you realize your limitations. Nut gathering is challenging work. Would you like a different job? I could use someone with tree climbing and vine swinging skills. I believe you would make a good message carrier."

I felt a little confidence returning. "Yes, that sounds like something I'm built to do!"

"You will take messages to field leaders in all harvest areas. You'll convey important changes in work plans and return with supervisors' responses. Effective communication is how we maintain production. Your ability to swing through widely spaced trees will avoid disruption to the valuable work of the gatherers. You'll connect my leaders to me."

I hoped to hear the ticking of my disk. Disappointed, I realized that this was only the beginning of the lesson—I had much more to learn before I could write.

I had been delivering messages for a few months before one day, as I swung between trees, I heard myself loudly humming the CNC tune. Grinning, I began to hum louder.

 Showing up and completing my task is a job. Fulfilling my purpose as part of a bigger goal is valuable work. That makes a real difference.

One afternoon JB called me to the office. "Pete, I have noticed how inspired you are in your work," he said sporting his usual smile, "Your innovative ideas are improving communication, and other messengers are willingly following you. That is leadership. I want to send you to advanced leadership training. Would you like to go?"

"Absolutely!" I said, excited.

"You will meet with your trainer Malc on Monday. Pay close attention and be sure to appreciate his passion. He has invested years developing leaders." JB patted me on the shoulder as he left.

Malc was an unassuming presence, hunched over from working every job at CNC. His eyes fell slightly below my chin. A kind voice was complemented by a face wrinkled from years of smiling, measuring time on his cheeks and forehead. He insisted on calling me Whippersnapper, but I didn't mind. The way he said it, it was a term of acceptance.

"Ok, Whippersnapper, let's see what you know," he said with a chuckle.

I unleashed what I felt were great words of wisdom, masterfully extracted from my travels and my limited exposure to leading. Malc leaned back, enduring my naive harangue.

"Well, that was a mouthful." His voice seemed more solemn now. "Let me start with some building blocks. A good foundation is key to growing as a leader." He spent the next few hours building a framework for development. Every point he made created anticipation for the next. By the end of our time together, which had been filled with questions, answers, scenarios, and role-play, my mind was saturated. And he had made a compelling case that there were no shortcuts. "Go home," he said. "Spend some time with your wife and kids." I definitely would. They renewed me.

And so began a very busy period for me, working as a messenger in the mornings and spending my afternoons with Malc, rarely having time for my family. I hadn't seriously looked for maize in months.

Chapter Seven

There was another face around the berm now. Lu had met a young dweller from a nice family. I needed to spend more time with him and clarify my role as her dad. I rehearsed in my mind how it would go: I would use my leader voice and set the rules.

Happily, that lecture was unnecessary. The young monkey's name was Oliver, and he gave me no reason for concern. Oliver had been raised in an exceptional family where he became a respectful and courteous adolescent. Already proving himself helpful around our berm, he rapidly became a nearly permanent fixture. And I chided myself: Instead of concern for Oliver's character, I should have had confidence in Lu's selection. Raising a family is similar to leading a team. Train them well and then trust that they will remember the foundational principles as they grow. I had not been objective. I had been looking through the wrong lens.

One day we took a family hike to the north, just east of CNC. We played a spying game to see who could find a plant that looked the most like maize. Oliver had a keen eye, so we had him lead. It was a good day. We stopped along the way to rest, eat, play, and laugh; however, we found only trees and open fields. No maize. The sun was moving into the west when Oliver spotted something far to the north. He called it a flicker. I looked for a painfully long time before my older eyes finally spotted it for myself.

"What do you think that is?" Oliver said.

"I'm not sure," I said. "It looks like something reflecting the sun. It has to be big." It seemed too close to be the City. But the appearance of the bright something to the north reminded me how late it had become. I rallied the family. "We need to go. It will be dark soon." We arrived home just as dusk fell across our berm. Too close for comfort.

The next day, Malc greeted me with an odd question. "Tell me something valuable you learned while you were spending time with your family." I spoke of our family's hunt for maize and Oliver's observation of the shimmering light to the north. "Very good," he said. "Now apply that to leadership."

I hadn't expected a test. I tried recalling lessons and insights Malc had shared, but somehow the story of my family's hike didn't seem to offer anything similar. Haltingly, I began: "I guess it was important that, uh, that it . . ." He waited while, embarrassed, I floundered in confusion.

Finally, mercifully, he interrupted. "This is the cornerstone of your foundation as a leader. Let's start with the easy part. Remember seeing JB standing in the fields with the workers?" I took in a breath to respond, but Malc didn't wait; he finished his point. "He models *important leadership* principles. Building a foundation as a leader requires four cornerstones. You already have the first cornerstone. It is your Faith. But to be an effective leader, you need to add three more: Vision, Inspiration, and Passion. A strong leader must be firmly anchored in all four to grow."

"How does that apply to my weekend?" I said, confused.

Malc ignored me as if I hadn't spoken. "First, you must provide vision to fulfill our purpose. Why do we do our work? I'm sure you noticed how all the gatherers hum the same tune, but have you noticed that all the polishers, packers, and even messengers also hum that exact same tune? That is the harmony of purpose. At home, it is how you work with Ellie to build purpose in unity to lead your family. Our workers understand that nuts are important to the City. They focus on purpose over task."

"Got it," I said, trying to recover from my loss of words earlier.

"Just listen," he said, his tone more stern now. "A leader must also motivate. Effective motivation comes through inspiration. Our inspiration at the CNC comes from JB. Inspiration brings into focus not just our purpose but the *intensity* of our purpose—why it's important, why it matters. JB makes sure each worker understands how we provide critical nourishment and medicinal resources for the citizens. It isn't just nut gathering. We save lives. JB inspires, and thus motivates, us all to remember that every day."

"Medicinal resources?" I said. "What do you mean?" Could this be somehow connected to the healing power of maize?

"They use nuts for some medicines in the City, but whatever use the nuts we harvest are put to, our role is the same—we harvest the nuts." Then he continued: "The final cornerstone is what drives you as the leader. It is passion. Workers connect to your vision and are inspired through your passion. Passion is what drives JB to work long hours, visit sick workers, volunteer at the town center, and still carve out enough time to value his family. I see passion in you, too, Pete. That is important leadership."

I asked him to wait a moment, pulled out my journal, and wrote down what I had just learned.

IMPORTANT LEADERSHIP:
Vision—Inspiration—Passion
- Vision—Fulfill my purpose by helping others become the greatest version of themselves.
- Inspiration—Motivate others to align in our purpose and to work and live in harmony.
- Passion—Nourish the earnest

> commitment that comes from within me. As a leader, I must understand our purpose, visualize the path to success, and lead with sincere passion.

"I understand, Malc," I said thoughtfully. Although he was applying *vision-inspiration-passion* leadership principles to my weekend, he didn't know I understood it as something much deeper. My vision to save Mom, Mags, and Lu had inspired my family to join me in searching the fields to the north when we moved to the Town. They had followed my passion and joined in our purpose.

Malc patted me on the head, "Pete, you're getting there. The real work is about to begin as you apply these principles to your journey."

Over the next weeks, I made a few more day trips east and northward but found nothing resembling maize. I longed for the ticking of my disk every day. My training with Malc complete, I was promoted to a new leadership position over production. Over the next year, I developed an amazing leadership team. I had their full support, and they stood by me faithfully. Much of my success came from standing on their shoulders. Trust and loyalty were the foundation of our relationship.

And after every harvest from our garden, I took home to Mom the bounty of our maize. She seemed preoccupied on those trips, but she continued to encourage me to continue my quest.

When I first met Meg, she was leading the line responsible for final preparation and storage. I admired how seriously she took her responsibility overseeing the team. It was her care and compassion that stood out to me the most—it was uncommon in the workplace to value people as much as process. Meg never forgot to consider the impact of management's decisions, even when her voice was alone in the room. In fact, I jokingly referred to her as *Three* because she was so often the odd one in the room.

I didn't fully grasp the impact Meg had on her team until one afternoon when one of our employees unexpectedly lost a family member. Before even going home to address her family crisis, that employee came to our workplace seeking Meg's support and counsel. Meg's solace brought that employee necessary comfort and peace to support their family in this crisis. That was compassion in action.

 Compassion—As a leader, I must take the time to understand and appreciate the impact of my decisions on a personal level. My sincere concern for my team unites us on an authentic and profound level.

Initially, I had questioned Meg's priorities as a production leader, but very quickly I realized the important balance she added to our team.

Our operation grew quickly, and that required more support staff. That brought Jan and Tim to our staff: Jan directed operations and Tim oversaw all labor-related activities. They aligned with Meg like strands of a cord with an unshakable bond. It was not uncommon to find one or all of them cleaning, serving a meal, or embarrassing themselves for the benefit of the team. I joined in as well. We were like family. Their authentic servants' hearts earned the admiration and respect of the entire operations group, especially JB.

This time, when my disk began to tick, I knew exactly what to add. Pulling the plank from its slot, I quickly etched **SERVICE** in the welcoming blue flames. Serving others above ourselves is important to cultivating a productive work culture.

Jan was a little fireball, with expectations rivaled only by her personal drive. She was fair, firm, and faithful. Her resolve was tested one summer when a storm seriously damaged our main packing area. The CNC leadership immediately started making plans to move to another permanent location, which could have uprooted families or caused people to lose their jobs. Jan was decisive—that could not be allowed to happen. She was able to relocate a portion of our team to a nearby temporary facility within a few days. They began producing immediately. Partnering with the Town leadership, Jan added more temporary space nearby and moved production to full capacity within a week. CNC would not have to move.

Jan's resolve provided the backbone for the new workplace, but she didn't do it alone. She had Tim at her side.

Tim took care of employee needs. I was amazed at how he could recall the names of hundreds of workers, and usually most of their family members, with ease. But his strongest attribute was offering guidance. He spent hours a day offering an objective ear.

I ran most of my employee decisions through the gauntlet of Tim's inquisition. He was my guardrail. He would say, "Peeeete," and then look at me without saying a word—but his expression clearly communicated that I might be steering in the wrong direction.

The value of this leadership team's friendship and support extended beyond CNC; it also reached into my family circle. My family had fallen into a comfortable routine. It was autumn, with Lu and Oliver getting married in a week. Meg, Jan, and Tim gave us the best gift. A surprise visit from Herman and Jo. They had heard me tell stories of Herman and his journey to the City. Working through CNC connections, they located Herman—and now here he was, with Jo, at our door.

"How have you been?" I shouted, hugging Herman's neck.

"He's been complaining about not seeing you," Jo said, smiling, "That's how he is."

Jo was particularly special to me. She and Herman had married almost immediately after high school, without a tree or vine to swing from. I admired the courage it took for them to forge a path for their lives beyond the Hedge. They were better together. Herman would not have made it out of the Community without Jo.

Pulling up a circle of chairs, I asked the question I'd been longing to ask him: "What about the City? Is it exactly as we always thought it would be?"

They told stories of life in the City. Bright beams of light, smooth shiny buildings, and stores on every corner. They described it exactly as I had imagined it.

"How far is it?" I asked, hoping it wouldn't involve overnight travel. I never forgot about the shadow beasts.

"A good day's walk," Jo said. "If you keep up your pace."

"We took two days getting here," Herman said. "Jo doesn't like my pace." He smirked. "There's a large medical treatment facility about half a day north of here—the Clinic. They have rooms for the families of their patients to stay overnight, and they allow travelers to stay a night or two."

The Clinic must have been the reflection Oliver saw on our family trip north, I thought.

"You can stay there when you come to see us," Jo nodded. "Now, let's talk about this wedding."

The next few days included lots of reconnecting, reminiscing, and laughing. Herman was a great storyteller, but to be honest, some of the stories he told of our childhood, I couldn't remember at all, or if I did, I remembered them differently. Still, it all felt familiar—it was a part of life that Herman and I had shared and that

I'll never again share with anyone else, since I'll never be that age again.

And now, providence had brought him back to me at this moment. I had no idea what was about to happen, but I would remember it all, in detail, for years to come. I was standing outside, between the berm and the garden. Herman and Jo were off visiting the Town; Jay and Emma had insisted on giving them a tour. Ellie was walking down the lane towards me. Her expression seemed lifeless, and I cocked my head—this was so unlike her. Something was very wrong. I walked to meet her. There were tears in her eyes. She slumped into my arms. We hugged for a long time, not saying a word—me because I had no idea what was wrong or what to say, and Ellie because she knew that her next words would change our lives forever.

"I'm sick," she said softly. "It's not good." Tears rolled down her cheeks. "I had my follow-up appointment with the doctor today, and he says I have a rare and terminal condition. They don't give me much hope."

Thoughts jumbled in my mind like lightning on a summer's eve: *This can't be happening. She's too young. We have a wedding in three days!* I pulled her even closer with a whisper, "We will get through this together."

We didn't tell anyone that night; we just went to bed. But there was no sleep for either of us. The silence of night was deafening as I stared at the sod above me. Thoughts of loss flooded my mind as water fills a lake. I desperately wanted to talk to her, but even though she was awake, I needed to leave her alone to maneuver sleepless waters of her own. I was overcome by sadness and fear. I couldn't allow myself to linger on thoughts of a future without Ellie. I kept thinking of Dad and how he leaned on his faith. Now I needed mine. There was a monster in the room with us now that made the creatures of the night outside seem small and impotent.

The morning brought a new light of hope. Coffee with Herman and Jo fueled the conversation as we shared the terrifying news.

"I'm so glad you are here," Ellie said weakly.

"Come on, Ellie—we can do this together." Herman's familiar phrase made me realize that fear was slicing into my root of faith.

"Yes, we can," I said, rising to my feet. Once again, I found myself trusting in the courage of my friend from the woods of my childhood.

"You remember that medical center where Jo and I stayed?" Herman said. "They have advanced medical treatment programs there. Jo and I will help you find someone there to help with your condition. Now let's celebrate love and a wedding."

We decided to not tell the kids until the next day.

We turned to the festivities and tried to forget about the cloud silently hanging over our family. The wedding day was perfect. We celebrated. I danced with the bride, Mom, Mags, and then my sweetheart. Mom had traveled to the wedding with friends from the Community. The trip was much easier now because someone had cut a large pathway through the Hedge in the spot where I had once bloodied myself crawling through.

A few days later Herman and Jo took us to the Clinic before heading home. Meg, Jan, and Tim managed the operation at CNC. JB monitored Ellie's and my status. The next few months were filled with long waits and the sound of doctors' voices, often obscured by the numbing fear that I might lose my best friend and life partner. I felt as though a hot rock was slowly migrating from my stomach to my head and back again. Our faith was an anchor, but I couldn't prevent the waves of fear from continually testing the strength of that faith. Jay and Emma, along with my leadership team, rallied dwellers and CNC workers who all wore wristbands in support. The bracelets read, "*BE STRONG AND COURAGEOUS.*" This was the fibrous root of community at work. We were not alone.

Unexpectedly, I found myself again wearing that dark suit that smelled a little funny. I held the hands of Mags and Lu, sensing that they were absorbing the finality of this moment. Words and flowers could not make up for a loss like this, regardless of the good intentions of the one offering them. We stood in the meadow where the Town held funeral services and buried its dead. I missed having Ellie's hand to hold. She would know the right words to say at a time like this. I didn't expect her health to fail so quickly—she was too weak to be with us.

The funeral was for a school friend of the girls. A dweller had found him a short distance from the berms with a bag of berries still in his hand. He must have found a patch late in the day and tried to haul an abundance back and then misjudged the time; darkness overcame him. We assumed the extra weight slowed him down. The shadow beasts took more than his life that night. Fear now grew like a fungus throughout the Town. I was especially careful to leave very early for the Clinic after that, allowing additional time for delays.

———•—•———

The morning of Ellie's big surgery had arrived. Ellie and I sat with the doctor as she explained the lengthy procedure and reminded us of the risks. Very few patients were afforded the opportunity to ring the bell signaling the end of a long successful fight. I kissed Ellie on the forehead and left the room, knowing that the odds of her surviving the day were not good.

The waiting room was lonely. I was mired in solitary thought. My children were with Herman and Jo. I had told them not to come until later. It was a long procedure, so there was no rush. But soon I wished they had come, because the first few hours became a struggle for sanity. Valiant attempts at hope would chase fear from one corner only to find despair looming in the other. I was cold—the kind of chill that fur couldn't remedy. Another round of echoing fears were about to begin their cycle when I heard a welcome voice. It was Emma.

She didn't leave my side. Soon other well-wishers and my family flooded the waiting room. Visitors came and went. Emma kept the conversation light as she made sure my family was positive and together.

That was the longest day. When Dr. Mason finally summoned us to hear the outcome, it was Emma who walked into the room with the kids and me. She asked the right questions, holding onto us the entire time. She was my rock through this storm. Thankfully, the news was better than expected. The procedure was a success. Even this long time later, I can recall many of Dr. Mason's exact words, because each one was precious to me.

After that, we made the unremarkable journey to the Clinic every week for six months. Dr. Mason had always been optimistic, but she never offered empty hope. She encouraged Ellie to have a positive attitude and to battle hard. Her positive attitude brought hope to the room. Remarkable as both a person and a physician, she was a ray of hope and constant encouragement. She taught us that attitude could dramatically impact the healing process. I will always recall her face the day she walked in with the news that all of Ellie's test results were good—she was getting better. I was gliding above the trees. Another tear rolled down Ellie's face—this time for joy. Ellie and I rang the bell together.

 When I was a small child, time seemed to pass at the pace of a snail. Days were long, nights even longer. Mischief had ample time to find me, and I was an eager participant in every adventure. I had nothing but time.

> As I grew into adolescence, I was
> impatient waiting for the passing sun to
> move me to my next big moment. Big things
> awaited me, and life was in the way. I needed
> time to move along.
>
> Adulthood added value to time. I realized
> that every minute must be used to the fullest.
> Time is how we mark moments of value in
> life. Time feels infinite, but life is not—it is
> terminable. Every moment of life is a gift.
> Celebrate often and celebrate loudly.

Finishing the entry, I could hear the long-awaited ticking in my pocket. "Finally" I said aloud. So much had happened since I last wrote on those coveted slivers of metal. I didn't know what to scribe. I thought of JB, Jay, Emma, Meg, Jan, Tim, the CNC workers, the dwellers, Herman, Jo and Dr. Mason. Then my thought became clear: Relationships had carried us through the Hedge to the Town and now to the Clinic. I pulled the plank away from the disk and scribed **RELATIONSHIPS**, rewarded with blue flames.

Chapter Eight

As soon as Ellie was strong enough, the family and I traveled to see Mom, excited to share the good news. Almost as if she were prescient, she was waiting on the porch. We laid the season's harvest on the porch and sat on the step. Things looked different. Had they changed, or was it me?

"I have good news," Ellie began with excitement. "Dr. Mason said I am getting better." She went on to explain in detail the events of the past months. I listened raptly; it was like hearing the good news for the first time again. Mom's joyous expression was as though she knew the end before Ellie had started the story.

"How have *you* been feeling, Mom?" I said as she gave Ellie a hug.

"I am so glad to see all of you," her face again taking on that serious look. "You have been away so long. There is something I need to share with you. I think you will understand now. It's the aerial root of our community tree. Think of it as a root that runs above the ground, connecting you to those outside the family. The root of fellowship is what you held fast to when you went beyond the Hedge. Your new shared experiences are the color of life." She stuck out her hand reminding me of our earlier lessons and extended her thumb followed by two fingers. "They are all connected. Faith, family, and now fellowship. When combined, they create harmony, support and peace."

An odd thought struck me. "Why isn't the disk ticking?" I asked. "This is important."

Ellie touched my knee and said, "Fellowship is a root of community and leadership; it should grow from within. It belongs in your heart."

I could see her point, but honestly, I think that all of the roots Mom had taught me so far—faith, family, and fellowship—should be taken to heart because they grow within us.

Though brief, this trip was filled with wisdom. We secured Mom with enough maize for another season and returned home. When I returned to work, the team was strong and our success was remarkable, but I began to feel empty, like still being hungry after eating.

It was another normal morning as JB approached with the news. "The City leadership asked me to have CNC host their annual business meeting. Our production and safety record impressed them, and they want to understand how we work here. Pete, I want you to lead the presentation"

I was nervous and excited at the same time. "We will shine, sir!"

Visitors from the City rarely visited our site. We had only a few weeks to prepare for this important meeting, and that required organization. I quickly created committees for decorations, entertainment, food, and cleaning. A *lot* of cleaning.

When we finished, CNC looked as much like a banquet hall as it did a factory. The night before the arrival of the delegation from the City, JB called a factory-wide meeting. I had helped him with his remarks and kept a draft to remind myself of the occasion:

> My friends, we are honored by this visit— honored that corporate leadership sees something in our production that they want to experience firsthand. They have monitored your record-breaking output and safety numbers for months. Each time, they ask if I think you can do more. They want to know our secret. I told them we work with purpose and do valuable work here. They are coming to observe for themselves. Tomorrow they plan to document amazing production strategies, process management, and quality control. Their hope is to take some of our success back to their plant in the City. I am confident they will see just that.
>
> They do not understand why we are successful. They don't yet grasp that our greatest resource is not our processes, but rather our team and service to others. I want you to come tomorrow as

yourselves. Don't pretend that you are something different. Let them see our amazing family as we are. We put a beautiful face on our buildings and are planning fun events, but that won't show them the secret to our success. That only welcomes them to our home. Let's show them CNC working with purpose. Thank you for all you do. Go home, rest, and let's have a normal day tomorrow.

Cheers erupted across the crowd. There were many with chests thrust out as though they had just received an award for employee of the year. JB had successfully personalized this visit, deferring credit for what our plant had accomplished to those standing in front of him. Our employees were our secret ingredient. That meant something.

I doubt many of the workers slept that night. We all anticipated the dawn like a birthday morning.

JB's comment about service really struck me. It was truly the indispensable ingredient of our success and the thing that united us. I stopped him as he was leaving. "Thank you, sir." He knew I was referring to more than the words of his speech.

I quickly wrote in my journal.

 Service puts others above self, with no job or person beneath me.

When the visitors arrived, employees greeted them with genuine smiles. Joy comes from within, and JB's speech the day before had left them with lots of it. Laughter and singing filled the air throughout the day. The visit felt more like a social event than a workday. Everything went as planned. I deployed diplomatic skills learned from my time with Dad, Malc, and JB. It became easier as I moved from one guest to the next. As the group was preparing to leave, the head executive asked me to report our production numbers for that shift. The executive's tone was skeptical as he asked, which made me suspect that if our productivity was down, he would somehow use that to deride our success. I asked for the shift report, confident that my staff would have the numbers readily available. Without even checking it, I placed it in his hand. Beads of sweat began forming on my nose as I watched his expressionless face.

"One hundred and twenty percent," he said with a slight smirk. "That's more production than you averaged for the month."

I thanked him for the visit and wished the delegation safe travels back to the City. I overheard a few of the executives on their way out talking about the culture here. They didn't seem to understand it, but recognized how engaged our employees were. The only way for them to quantify what had organically grown in this workforce was to look at the production numbers, and that dramatic increase was a result of authentic leadership and tireless investment in the team.

Culture—It is hard to document success that is realized through organic growth stemming from authentic leadership. I must replicate the atmosphere and maintain the culture. Processes are how we work; however, workplace culture is how well we work together.

Soon after their visit, JB asked me to walk with him. I knew this was more than a stretch of the legs. We sat on a gravel bar next to a stream. The icy-cold water ran swiftly as small fish cruised along the rapid undercurrent. Most of them battled mightily to gain only a short distance in order to take a nibble of a lone strand of water weed flapping in the current. JB pointed out that their struggle was similar to Ellie's and my recent battle with her health. He asked about her and the kids, then spent some time reflecting on his time as a leader. We paused and watched the water pass in restful silence.

"You made quite an impression, Pete." JB looked me dead in the eye, his expression melancholy. "The City leaders asked me to transfer you to their operations. It will be a role in the Tower. That's a big career step. I'm proud of you." His eyes drifted back to the stream.

Trying to control my surge of emotion, I softly replied, "Sir, I am honored to work for you and would be proud to represent you in the City. Do you think I can do it?"

"Pete," JB replied after an uncomfortable silence, "the question is never *if* you can do something, but rather *how* you can do something. Appreciate that difference—it is critical to success. Trust your resources and instincts."

Thank you, Sir, was on the tip of my tongue, but the mood suggested that I remain silent.

JB leaned toward the water. "Stay in touch. Remember, relationships extend beyond physical connection." He gently pressed his hand into the sifted gravel at the water's edge. The sandy slush retreated from the light pressure of his touch. "What is a leader's role?" he asked.

My heart began to race again. This was a final test. I scrolled through mental files looking for the right words. How could I weave Malc's teachings on leadership into this answer? My palms were sweaty.

JB leaned back and broke the silence: "Look where my hand was. My hand is no longer there, but you can still see how it changed the shape of the sand. Wherever you go, whoever you meet, one thing you can't avoid is leaving an impression. Be cognizant of your impact on your surroundings."

"Is the purpose of leadership leaving an impression?" I asked.

"Not exactly," he replied. "Leadership is influence. Great leaders have vision, they listen and they unite; but most importantly, they build energy around purpose. They influence others to be their best and work together as a team."

It made sense. JB had been influencing me since my arrival at CNC—by encouraging me to become objective, to be empathetic, and to lead.

JB stood, threw a pebble into the stream and strolled away in thought. That was his way of releasing me.

Leaving the office that day felt like a parade; those who had helped me along my journey at CNC were strategically staged along the path I walked as I left the building to say a few words to encourage me as I approached my next frontier. JB was resolute in his commitment to leadership development right down to the last day. I respected that, but mostly I admired him because he reminded me of my dad.

"And Dad would approve of this," I whispered to myself. I realized that, if I saw images of Dad in JB, I saw them in myself as well.

Walking home, I anticipated the ticking before my ears actually detected it. I knew exactly what to write about how a leader unites others through vision, inspiration, and passion. I etched **_INFLUENCE_** into the welcoming blue flames.

The next few days were difficult. Ellie and I spent hours wrestling with our choices. Since the beginning of our marriage, we always made a pros-and-cons list whenever we faced a big decision. We did so this time, too, but one thing that became clear is that, if I was to take the offered position in the City, there was no easy way to accomplish that for our family. Besides the usual problems of uprooting kids from friends and school, we also had to continue to supply my mom's need for maize.

The most sensible option would be for me to leave Ellie and the family in the Town while I ventured to the City. I could temporarily live with Herman and Jo, who had offered their spare room any time I needed it. Ellie and the kids would keep maize growing in the garden. I had never left my family alone before. My travels home would be infrequent—realistically, one or two times a month.

The guilt I felt about this was so overpowering I was on the verge of deciding to refuse the promotion when I heard Ellie's sweet voice say, "I am proud of you." That was all I needed to hear. We hugged each other one last time, and I left for the City.

I had packed lightly in order to make the full journey in one day. I left early, passing the berms of the town until all I could see was open field. Soon, I could no longer hear the sounds of the Town at all. I traveled the better part of a day before I could see the familiar images of the Clinic. We had been there too often, but familiarity made this part of the trip easier. With the midday sun just beginning to pass over my head, I paused for a minute. *Should I stay for the night?* I wondered. I decided to continue, but I soon began second-guessing myself, and my anxiety grew with each step as the Clinic fell far behind me.

It was a hot day, and I stopped frequently for long drinks from my water jug. The sun seemed to be racing me now. Even with my best effort, I was losing speed. Besides that, things felt oddly out of place. As the long afternoon waned, the sun began to settle toward the horizon more quickly. The temperature hadn't dropped, and I had been walking in the direct sun for most of the afternoon. My supply of water was now totally gone, and I was very thirsty.

"Trees! Where are the trees?" I said aloud, just to hear a voice. The path led now through large open fields of stumps, as though someone had cut all the trees down in one swing. And there were strange tracks in the dirt—holes evenly spaced in rows running together in one direction. As I moved between stumps, I took a close look at each track. They all looked exactly the same. But as I squinted toward them, trying to decide what had made those tracks and why, it struck me suddenly that it was getting dark, and that's why it was difficult to see. My delays in the heat, complicated by my increasing dehydration due to my foolishly inadequate supply of water, had kept me from reaching the City before nightfall. And there was no shelter in sight.

"You need to find a tree fast!" I shouted at myself. But surveying the broken forest in all directions, I could see only short stumps and random piles of limbs. Except—in the dimming light, on a hill far across a deep valley, stood two solitary trees. I walked toward them as quickly as I could, hoping not to draw attention to myself. If shadow beasts ranged this far north, I didn't want to give them an invitation. My pack now felt heavier than before. My legs weakened with every frightful step, and I knew I was stumbling more often than I would have had I not been so dehydrated. My head pounded. Except for my own footsteps in the dust, it was eerily quiet—until I heard sticks crack to my left. I shot a look in that direction but didn't stop for even a second.

My steps were now so clumsy that I had to slow my pace or fall. I clambered down to the bottom of the ravine that stood between me and the two trees that I hoped would be my salvation. The other side was much steeper than I had anticipated. Within a few steps up, I was on my hands and knees grabbing for clumps of grass, rocks, or roots, whatever I could use to pull myself up toward the safety of the trees, which were faintly visible in the moonlight—and they were still so high above me. *How can I make this climb?* I wondered, but a moment later I discovered my motivation—a sinister sound echoing through the valley. The beasts had found me! I threw off my pack and frantically scrambled up the ravine wall, slipping back about half the distance gained on every lunge. I was terrified. The baying of the beasts was closer now. The only heartening thing was that none of their sounds came from in front of me, but I could hear more than one source from behind, as well as a scratching sound made, I imagined, by sharp claws on rock and root. In less than a minute, their sounds were coming from not just behind me but from both sides as well, and they were moving much faster than me.

The two trees, as it turned out, were growing from a steep, crumbling hillside. Still, what a relief to reach the base of the first tree! I pulled myself upright and reached for a limb, only to find nothing but the smooth surface of the trunk on every side. With the crying of shadow beasts only a few feet away, I desperately scrambled for the second tree, hoping to find a branch or vine to climb to safety. Then came a terrifying scream from my right, and I looked that way just in time to see long sharp teeth lunging in my direction. I shouted as loudly as I could, wishing I had the noisemaker that Jay had used in our garden, and thrust my right arm out to protect myself. Sharp pains raced through my arm as the night creature clamped on with incredible strength. Holding fast to an exposed tree root with my free hand, I kicked at the hairy beast, and connected too, but its teeth seemed to dig deeper with every blow. Summoning all my strength, I made one final push, lifting my body as I swung my bloody arm into the air, still holding the root with the other. The steep incline gave me an advantage, and the beast lost footing and fell further below.

My right arm hung like a rag. Pushing myself up with my legs, I used my left hand to pull my way up the root. I was able to scramble to the base of the second tree by the time the second shadow beast reached me. This one didn't scream, but I knew it was there by its overpowering smell. I was being stalked; it was just waiting for the right moment to pounce. I discovered that what I had thought was a root was actually a vine attached to the tree. I tightened my grip and began to swing side to side, arcing out over the void. I hit a limb with my shoulder, which pushed me back, but I realized, *You can swing out over the*

valley and grab that limb with your legs as you come back.
The stealthy beast chose his moment—he let out a spine-freezing scream and leapt toward me. I was far past the point of timidity if I wished to survive. I jumped directly at him and pressed my foot into the tuft of fur above its yellow eyes. Pushing with all the strength of my legs, using his head as an unwilling support, I swung over the valley, picked up speed, and slammed into the base of the tree with great force. Breathless and bruised, I desperately wrapped my legs around the trunk.

No good—I immediately began to slide toward the ground. And then my left foot felt the safety of a limb. My head against the trunk of the tree, I straddled the thick limb.

I didn't have the luxury of simply resting—I had to make sure I was safe. I looked around in the moonlight. The steep hillside leveled off just above the spot that the tree grew out of the ground, so I was high enough above the shadow beasts to be safely out of their reach until morning. I took a quick inventory: I was tired and bleeding, but alive.

After that assessment, I simply clung to the tree and tried to catch my breath for a long, long time. When I was finally capable of thought again, my first one was: *Won't I have a story to tell Jay next time I see him!*

Morning brought perspective to my pain. My right forearm had two deep gashes where the beast's teeth had torn at my flesh. I had slept little, and I was exhausted. With the sun rising to my right, I could now see just over the hill ahead of me. Almost as far as I could see, there were fields filled with rows of plants. Just beyond the fields was a giant glowing image of magnificence. I had found the City.

Lowering myself to the ground, I backtracked to my pack and empty water bottle, both still intact. After wrapping my arm with a piece of cloth from my pack, I crawled back to the top of the hill. A short walk later I was standing at the edge of a massive sea of tall golden stalks of maize. With a grateful sigh, I dropped to my knees in awe.

These were big stalks, taller than me. I wanted to run back and tell Ellie, but first my arm needed care before it became infected. I pressed into the maze of stalks. Plant after plant, row after row, the view was the same. I couldn't find my way. The ground was covered with the same familiar tracks I'd seen yesterday, with equally spaced holes. Since I couldn't see ahead or behind, I decided to follow the tracks. After a long walk, I was at the opposite edge of the field looking up at the majesty of the City.

 Set my eyes on the path that leads to my objective, and keep them there. Without setting a course and maintaining focus on the plan, I will wander without direction.

I decided to not search for Herman's home yet—my arm needed care first. I walked into The City. The sun was now fully above the horizon as I stepped past the first building. Everything was shiny, reflecting brightly at every turn. Disoriented, I stumbled over a long rock somehow fastened to the ground. Trying to get to my feet, I was almost crushed by an enormous hairy animal ambling down the pathway. The surface below me felt odd to the touch. It was hard and warm, not like dirt paths in the forest. This strange surface amplified the sound of steps. The long solid rock purposely outlined the edges, making neat rows of strangely smooth ground. My left hand now pulsed with pain, and I saw that I'd gotten a small cut when I'd tripped.

Animals were racing toward me from every direction. A voice broke my daze: "Get out of the way!" It came from a very tall, furry animal in a big hurry. Everyone seemed to be. Small round circles of frozen water were hanging over both of the tall animal's eyes as he stared at me with both hands in the air and an odd expression. He was looking at me, but it was as though he could not see me. He didn't stop or acknowledge my existence, other than making it clear that he wanted me to move. One after another, I encountered animals, almost all wearing circles over their eyes while walking briskly, and almost all with both hands raised. This was worse than crushball. Dodging back and forth, I finally found safety under a tall, metallic, tree-like structure. I needed to find a way through this sea of animals without being mashed into that hard surface they traveled across. The cold metal structure I sheltered under looked enough like a tree that I decided to climb. That was difficult with my injured right arm, but I made it as high as the first set of metal vines that stretched from this structure to other similar structures. I heard an unpleasant screeching, and in the distance, I spotted the source. A female animal of some kind was coming my way. She wore a funny hat over her gray furry head and had a flashing light on her chest. Now she had made it to the base of my metal tree, and she continued her rant—obviously agitated with me.

I could hear her now: "Stop, get down from there!"

Trying to steady myself, I reached for the vine with my good hand—and a sudden hot pain burned my feet.

Chapter Nine

The smell of burnt fur and alcohol welcomed me back to reality. Everything was fuzzy. I heard voices, but they were distant and faint. Some words made sense while others were long and confusing. I could tell they were talking about me.

Something tall and wearing white said, "What would make a monkey try to climb a plantology pole? Surely he knew the danger." Everything seemed shiny or white. I was about to ask what plantology was when I realized the burnt fur smell was coming from my body. I was in excruciating pain. My skin hurt as though I was trapped in the thicket of the Hedge. Each movement increased the pain's intensity.

A kind voice interrupted my agony. "Well, hello. How are you feeling today?" Her voice was sweet like Mom's. I heard another voice call her Helen. She seemed to be a physician's assistant like the ones we had met at the Clinic.

"Helen," I said, "can you explain what plantology is?"

"You don't know—but wait—let's start with your name." She seemed surprised.

"My name is Pete. I'm from the Town. I transferred here to work at the Tower. Please explain what plantology is."

"You are new here indeed," she said. "Plantology is what creates spark. Don't ask me to explain the process, but they take maize and turn it into spark which gives us power. Spark flows across the metal lines, like the one you touched. They are very dangerous. You are fortunate to be alive."

"Do you use maize for anything else?" I asked, thinking of Mom.

"Yes, almost all of our food and some medicine comes from maize," Helen said. "Over the years we have cut down much of the forest to make room to grow more maize. We also stopped growing most other plants. Maize is the source of life, and plantology is the conduit of life-giving energy in the City."

Helen went on to explain that the City was much more sophisticated than the Town, something of which she seemed very proud. She had never even heard of the Community. Plantology offered a doorway to endless possibilities, she said. Now I understood why there had been only stumps where I'd encountered the shadow beasts the night before.

When she had finished explaining plantology, she reached into her pocket and pulled out wire-framed ice circles, like the ones others had been wearing out on the street. Then she tapped her hands together and raised them into the air.

"What is that on your face?" I asked.

"They're called clarifiers. We wear them to use our MEVEDs. Before you ask, that stands for Mobile Eye Voice and Ear Device." She took her clarifier off, placed it over my eyes and removed two hoops, one each from the first finger on each hand. She then slipped the small hoops over the first finger on each of my hands. The one on my right hand really hurt, but I didn't tell her. "Now clap your hands together gently and lift your arms."

I clapped my hands, but she had to help me lift my right arm. The clarifiers had been clear until I clapped my hands. When I lifted my arms, I could see a yellow box of color between my hands. I could still see through the clarifiers but not very well. Helen pressed my hands together again, and my clarifiers became clear.

"Your screen was blank because you don't have a PIN, which is a Plantology Information Node."

"How do I get a PIN?" I asked eagerly. I wanted one right away.

"It takes training before you can have one. You start by wearing pre-programmed clarifiers that have information you need to do your job. After you master that you can request a PIN to be installed, below the skin, behind your ear. It keeps all the information you need to do your task and is in continuous contact with the Tower. I'm sure you'll get a clarifier when you start your new job. Now get some rest."

She was out of the room before I could ask anything further.

Over the next few days, as I was recovering, I learned about the City. They had a leader, called the overseer, who was selected by the citizens every two years. Citizens are what they called the animals who lived in the City. The leadership had a group of thinkers who worked in the Tower. They created plantology and made most decisions and rules for the City. Since the discovery of spark, the City had become bright day and night. Clinic hallways were filled with PAWs, or Powered Artificial Workers, who scurried constantly around hallways. PAWs were able to do so much more work than animals; even those like Helen who had important jobs, spent most of their time looking at MEVEDs and resting.

As soon as I could get out of bed, I went to see Herman and Jo. They lived on the west side of town very close to a maize field. As I approached, Jo was planting flowers in front of their home. She was a welcome sight.

"Pete! You made it!" she shouted as she rushed in to get Herman. They both greeted me at the door. After the hugs and when they had shown me what would be my room, we sat while I explained my new position, the trip here, the dangerous encounter with the shadow beasts, and what I had learned about plantology and the City.

"Well, somebody's done a good job of bringing you up to speed," Herman said with a smile. "You can figure the rest out as you go." Herman had a job in his sector—designated groups of homes within the City. He was responsible for his sector's use of maize and for rule violations. That connected him to key people in the City's leadership.

I knew I was welcome to stay with Herman and Jo as long as I needed, and I was grateful for their friendship and hospitality. Looking out their window just then, I saw PAWs weaving almost in unison across the fields of maize. I looked at Jo and said, "Tell me about the PAWs. How are they able to work in the maize?"

"They run on hard flat continuous treads with sharp cleats to help with traction," she said. "They need no rest, so PAWs run day and night."

That explains the holes in the dirt that led me to the City. "How do I get maize that I can take back to the Community?" I said casually. They didn't know of the severity of Mom's condition, so I acted as though I was thinking of it only for food.

"Don't say that too loudly," Herman said. "They take maize very seriously around here. You can't take any out of the City. Not even if you find it in a field that the PAWs have finished harvesting. PAWs work in the fields alone, without human oversight—mainly for that reason. Taking maize is a serious offense."

"Do they allow you to grow it for yourself?" I asked, hoping I could grow some to help with Ellie's harvest.

"None," Jo said. "*All* maize must be brought to the Tower. No exceptions."

I didn't press any further. This was clearly a sensitive topic, and I didn't want to put Jo and Herman in an awkward position. It seemed unfair that I wasn't able to take some of this bounty of maize to Mom. However, I was encouraged that it grew so far north. Perhaps my excursions would eventually uncover crops outside the City.

We spent the rest of the evening sharing stories of our childhood. We laughed until it was time to sleep.

As soon as the sun's light touched my window the next morning, my feet hit the ground. On my way to the Tower, I was able to avoid being crushed on the busy streets while marveling at the different animals and their colorful clothes. Many of them wore big hats. I could have spent hours just watching them, but I had an important place to be. I passed rows of majestic structures projecting long shadows along the walkway. Herman had called them buildings the night before. At last I found the courtyard nuzzled against a series of massive white buildings. A large sign hung over the courtyard entry: *The Tower*. Tall round pillars encircled a bright sky-scraping structure resembling maize. I had finally arrived: My first day in my new role working for the Tower. Reaching the gates was a breeze; however, getting past the administrator who guarded them, not so much. He was a small hairy animal with tiny clarifiers worn low on his nose. His name was Ronald, and he spoke slowly and methodically, making me feel like a child in school.

"State your business." His voice was firm and unwelcoming.

"I am Pete from CNC. I was transferred to work for the Tower."

He seemed to be expecting me, smiling slightly with his tiny sharp teeth. "Follow me." He spun around and quickly moved through the gates. Inside were colorless rooms housing animals quietly staring through their clarifiers. They weren't holding their hands up for some reason. It looked as if they were reading images projected on the tops of their tables. It was quiet, nothing like CNC. Ronald took me down a long hallway to a small office where he introduced me to Leon, the director of maize conversion. Leon followed the direction of the overseer.

Leon was much taller than me because of his extremely long neck, and his thinness made him appear even taller. He stood in a way that took advantage of that height and seemed designed to make me feel inferior. His spindly body matched his lean personality. Later, I would learn that he was fond of regaling the team with unbelievable stories of his importance and stature, as though he alone provided the food and spark for the citizens. My co-workers had secretly given him the name *Peebow*—short for "Pompous Bag of Wind," but I thought it more appropriate to show him the respect of his position.

Leon shut the door. "This is very confidential," he began in a solemn tone. "You were brought here to improve efficiency in maize conversion. Citizens are consuming more maize than we can grow."

"Why not cut back on the consumption?" I asked.

"Not a chance! Maize conversion creates plantology which creates power for MEVEDs and PAWs. It also gives power to the overseer. Whoever owns the power of plantology runs the City."

I was confused, "What do you mean by control?" I was serious, but Leon didn't take it that way. He chuckled.

"Don't think you can fool me by playing the innocent, Pete. I know you're here to move up the ladder. You want to be in a position of power one day just like the rest of us. Figure out how to improve conversion efficiency, and you will move up fast."

It seemed like a good fit, since I had managed production workers at CNC for years. Their processes here in the City were, to my surprise, antiquated; they needed refinement. But the team itself was strong, lacking only in leadership. There was some tension at first, as the team's pride rejected new ideas. I focused on simple successes, creating momentum to tackle the more difficult challenges. Team chemistry grew like plants to a gardener's touch. I was expecting the process to take months instead of weeks, but to my surprise, I quickly had the team ready for Leon's vision and growth.

But I soon learned that Leon was not that kind of leader. He was not like JB at all. He seemed completely disinterested in my leadership or ideas. His vision was for me to do exactly what he said and to not ask questions. When my team had an idea, Leon would take it to the Tower and present it to the overseer—as his own idea. I told myself that this is what gave him such a long neck: His self-image convinced him that he belonged at the top level of the Tower, while his lack of ability prevented him from ascending there. We could not grow with Leon at the helm of the department.

I was contemplating my next approach to Leon when the disk began to tick. *What have I learned here? Certainly not to emulate Leon's disingenuous approach to leadership.* What I had observed in him had no place on one of the disk's planks. I stared at the plank for a long time before it occurred to me to consider how I should perform in my own role regardless of how Leon performed in his. I wrote **INTEGRITY** on the plank. Relishing the blue flames of acceptance, I placed the disk back in my pocket and vowed to treat this new job with integrity regardless of how others acted. I wrote in my journal for reference, as I anticipated the need to remind myself of integrity again in the near future.

 As a leader I must be honest, honorable, and sincere to earn the trust and respect of those I lead. I must enable my team by removing obstacles while promoting innovative thinking. Group success far exceeds my individual gain or recognition.

A few weeks later, I traveled back to see Ellie and the family. I made sure to leave early, and as I walked, I paid special attention to the sun and water breaks. As a result,

I had a much less stressful trip and arrived well before sundown. The harvest was complete, and Ellie was ready to travel to the Community with me. I told her all about the City during our walk.

It didn't take us long, after we arrived, to realize that Mom was distracted. She had a large group of dissimilar animals working around her yard building contraptions. I didn't pay much attention to them at first, but then I noticed Mom's body language—she was anxious and impatient. Still, she took a few minutes to sit and sip some freshly brewed coffee with us. We chatted about city life and what I had learned along the way.

She looked at me intently and said, "Have you been writing in the disk?"

"Yes. The truths have been random, but they're still important."

She stopped for a moment and stared at the trees. Lowering her cup, she asked, "What kind of leader will you become?" When I didn't respond, she said, "You've described your journey and the City, but you haven't told me what you will do in your new role. Who is Pete the leader?" She excused herself and joined the animals in her yard.

I took her question to bed with me, mulling it over all night. Mom's home was usually a refuge of peace and quiet, but her question had made me feel tired and perplexed. I longed for the energy and brilliance of city life, where I could expand my responsibility and grow my influence. I thought about her question for our entire journey back to the Town and also as I walked back to the City. I couldn't shake the thought of the ominous responsibility of the leader.

———•◦•———

In the City, improvement in production was difficult to achieve at first, as I tried to deploy proven tactics from previous roles. I took a pause and observed the entire operation from a holistic view. It was like watching a dysfunctional hive. There was no order, only mayhem. Remembering Dad's magnet lesson gave me ideas for a new approach. My team needed support and understanding, not a strong force pushing for a new and unfamiliar solution. I had to calm the noise and align the team.

I called them together and drew a simple chart on the wall. "You have the skills and abilities to succeed," I said calmly to open the meeting, "What I am observing is chaos and confusion. Disruptions are neither effectively addressed nor communicated to the appropriate levels." I had their attention. "We need to acknowledge what is within our control, what is out of our control, what we influence, and what influences us before we can make an effective strategic plan." Pointing to the drawing on the wall, I said, "This chart will help us address the havoc on our work floor. Using this method, we will agree on the top three opportunities for a more efficient and effective operation, develop improvement steps, understand how to measure success, and move from confusion to structure."

I had already drawn the chart in my journal.

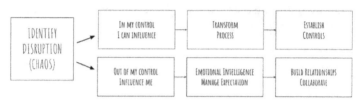

The team began to apply the simple flow. Quickly agreeing on innovative ideas and improvements, we identified communication as the root cause of the problem. Some leaders were diving too deeply into details while others were ignoring the need for direct, two-way dialog with those who reported directly to them. We needed to clarify key objectives with precise and focused communication.

Together we wrote a summary of what we'd learned. I added it to my journal.

 Details are critical but must be simplified as we communicate up the levels of oversight. Every level of leadership must effectively summarize critical metrics for the next-level leader. The most senior leader should receive a valuable synopsis of the health of the entire operation.

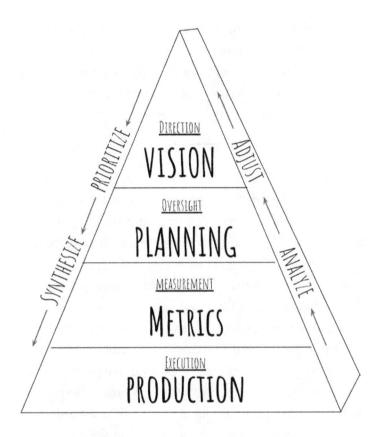

The impact was almost immediate. Normally exhausted from working overwhelming hours, the team was now rejuvenated. Spirits rose along with productivity. I supported my team's new ideas, and they put them into practice. The key was for me to not involve myself in the details, and to trust my managers to handle the details themselves. That one change alone was critical to developing confidence and success in my leaders. Within weeks, we had successfully implemented employee engagement strategies, such as including workers in many decisions. We were now celebrating, together, even small successes. The entire team began to believe. Smiles slowly returned, as though a steady rain was falling on a dry field.

Maize conversion improved by ten percent.

———•◦•———

Though exhausted, I traveled back to Ellie and the kids. We had added another gift to our lives: Ash, my grandson, who had eyes like stars in a dark sky. Freshly buttered bread couldn't compete with the satisfaction and warmth of his hug. His energy and giggles brought happiness to the worst day. I was immediately refreshed. We packed maize, Oliver, Lu, and Ash before heading back to the Community to introduce him to Mom.

The atmosphere at Mom's was distinctly different from our last trip. Now there was a carnival-like feeling. Mom had assembled a band of misfits to work on a secret project, and I couldn't recall seeing so many animals united in purpose. I inquired about the purpose, but she was a vault. Her reply, "All in due time, my son," was simply annoying.

We spent a week there to allow her time with Ash. The army of animals worked tirelessly that whole time. There were carts, tents, and supplies strewn over the ground, as though we were going on a community camping trip. I helped build some wooden boxes, enjoying the memory of working with my hands. This group reflected the passion of the Community, something I had just begun to feel connected to again when the time came to return to my job at the Tower.

We hugged Mom goodbye and walked away past swinging hammers, canvas, and wood piles. Approaching the Hedge, I felt a weight around my waist, as though something was pulling me back. Was there some important task I should stay and complete? Whatever it was, I was too eager to return to the City and continue the success my team had been experiencing there to spend any longer in the Community; I kept going.

It wasn't until I had deposited Ellie and the kids back home and was on my way back to the City that I realized Mom and I had not had our usual cup of coffee together. I felt a brief pang of sadness but pushed any sense of guilt for not initiating it out of my mind.

———•◦•———

The City was changing. The population had been growing rapidly, and to accommodate the newcomers, new buildings and roads had been constructed. This rapid growth required even more resources. Maize, spark, PAWs, and MEVEDs were running low. Violations of rules, like theft, began to rise. Animals were hoarding their resources, and some were stealing from others. It was as though, overnight, paradise had turned to pandemonium. Interviews and comments from angry citizens filled the MEVEDs. Civility decreased as resources were depleted. Factions developed: Many lost trust in the overseer while others fiercely defended city leadership. The streets seemed darker as civil debate gave way to angry tirades.

The time for citizens to select the next overseer arrived in the midst of this turmoil. The election process took three painful months. Families fought and refused to speak to each other. I couldn't bear reading the news reports on my MEVED. The rhetoric was depressing. Not only were we running low on resources, we were also running out of courtesy for other citizens.

One eventful afternoon summarized the mood perfectly. It was Maize Days, an annual celebration of the development of plantology. Traditionally, this was a fun day centered in the parks, which were filled with picnics, music, and children playing. This year was an exception. Tension had grown to a fevered pitch. Signs and placards replaced tents and picnic tables. Loud groups of unhappy citizens marched through fields where, in a normal year, children usually flew kites. Long, angry speeches replaced joyful music from the stage. Something had changed, and not for the better. The fight over the selection of the new overseer was becoming more violent than simply the angry chatter between two factions—it threatened to tear the City in two.

Eventually, though, Election Day passed. The new leader's name was Jimmy. I was surprised at his appearance. I had never before seen so much color and fanfare in an animal. His large tail feathers plumed with the colors of the rainbow. I soon learned that Jimmy was all about appearance; he cared more about how others viewed him than he cared for others. Despite having little leadership experience, he now sat in the Tower perched at the top of the City.

And it was both unsettling and exciting that I was on his staff.

Chapter Ten

One by one, Jimmy called the leaders who answered to him into his office and asked us a series of pointed questions. We called our departure from his office after those interviews the walk of shame, because some left with a look of shock and others dejection. After each meeting, I would hear Jimmy working with Ronald to add to the list of those who would soon be leaving his staff. It appeared that agreeing with him was the only way to keep your job. I survived my inquisition and kept my head down, trying not to make waves while meeting his demands.

Jimmy wasn't shy. He frequently simply stated how brilliant he thought he was, an opinion not shared by most of the team. Stating ideas that differed from Jimmy's resulted in a booming rebuttal, forcing the speaker to submit and ultimately to abandon his "rebellious" idea. Jimmy's leadership style was so self-absorbed that it reminded me of a room full of mirrors. He refused to entertain advice from anyone who thought differently from him.

Trying to survive in that pressure-cooker had a profoundly negative impact on me and on the rest of our team. And when I heard the ticking of my disk, I knew exactly what it beckoned me to record. I wrote **HUMILITY** in welcoming flames. A true leader demonstrates humility, especially in success.

The City continued to grow, as did the shortages of food and services. Finding qualified labor was one issue, but the overconsumption of maize was a bigger problem. We weren't producing enough, and our fields were becoming overworked. Crop yields declined as vital nutrients were not allowed time to replenish in already exhausted soil.

Jimmy's response? He recorded a video message to play on all MEVEDs. In the video, he looked calm and relaxed, sitting in front of a beautiful field of maize.

"It's a great day to live in the City." He started every public message with that line. "I am excited to announce the approaching completion of our next phase of plantology. With recent breakthroughs, we will soon increase production of spark. This will leave more for food consumption. While we complete this final and important phase, I ask all citizens to ration their use of maize by half. We will turn spark off during certain hours and reduce citizen portions from the supply siloes. With your help, we will make our city even greater. Thank you for supporting the expansion of knowledge and plantology."

As soon as the video appeared, Jimmy called a meeting of the senior leadership. "Our shrinking food supply is at a critical level. We must find new sources of maize in the next months or we will be forced to ration supplies even more. We are unable to sustain the growth in our population without more maize."

A voice called from the middle of the room: "What about the next phase of plantology?" Dale, the director of plantology research, was a well-respected leader of academia, known for being steady and being an exceptional thinker. Although he was reserved in manner, his words were always worth hearing. He continued: "It seems to me we have a problem involving the entire city, and in my opinion that requires a well-coordinated response and an advancement in our current plantology programs. I am unaware of a new phase in our research. Can you enlighten me?"

There is an eerie feeling just before a big thunderstorm. The air feels heavy, almost like wearing another coat of fur. Birds stop singing and the forest falls silent and still. At that moment you expect savagery from the sky. Wise animals find shelter. The atmosphere in the room was exactly like that.

Jimmy plumed his feathers in obvious annoyance. "We will take a five-minute break while Ronald and I speak with Dale." His voice was sinister, but tranquil.

All of us but Dale filed out of the room. Five minutes turned into an hour. Eventually we were called back into the room where Jimmy continued his comments as though nothing had happened. And all of us were well aware that Dale was not there.

"The fields are no longer sufficient to feed our growing population. I am sending a scouting expedition eastward, through the forest, to find new fields of maize. We will announce and promote it as a big event to excite the citizens about the next phase. I will tell them we have found additional resources and are sending a team to determine the best way to harvest them. This will help with morale and give us time to find other sources to generate spark. I have selected a leader, and he has already chosen his team."

The leader's name was Kip. He was shorter than I and had a kind face and red fur. He always smiled, but his teeth appeared razor sharp. He announced the members of his team, my name among them. And I was excited to be included. This would be the challenge of a lifetime. We were on a quest to save the citizens.

Before our departure, Kip called each of us into his office individually. When my turn came, he welcomed me in and asked about my family and also my adventures. I thought that an odd way to prepare for such a significant journey, but I was happy to share. He identified with many of my stories. Five years earlier, he had come to the City, and like me, he had worked hard in the hope of earning a place on the senior leadership team. He now carried the future hope of an entire city. We actually spoke very little about the task ahead of us, other than a short conversation about packing requirements, my role, and our departure time.

I was to be the scout—chosen, I assumed, because my ability to move from treetop to treetop with speed and ease would offer Kip a better perspective of the unknown landscape ahead. Kip had found a kind black-and-white furry cook to prepare meals, a hoofed animal to carry our load, and two strong protectors. To Jimmy's displeasure, Kip gave us time to travel home and see our families before we departed.

———•◦•———

Ellie had prepared another harvest of maize, so in the short time I had, we traveled back to the Community together. I told Mom about Jimmy, the shortage of maize, and our mission to search the east for additional supplies.

My offer for her to stay with Ellie for a while was politely rebuffed. "We have all we need in the Community. Right now, we need to prepare for what is to come," she said, pointing to the east. I looked up and saw nothing but sky and trees. I did notice, though, that the number of animals surrounding her home had grown again. There were now tents in the yard and temporary structures being built nearby.

"Why are all of these animals around your home?" I asked, frustrated that the presence of all of these animals, and the responsibility to make sure that they were sheltered and fed, was taking its toll on Mom's strength.

She was kind as usual. "You'll understand soon enough."

Ellie and I headed back to the Town the next morning, busily discussing my imminent journey and Mom's inscrutable comment. I stayed at the berm a few more days, then walked back to the City, spending the night at the Clinic this time, to reserve my strength.

Our team—six nervous animals hoping to survive a journey into unknown forests of mystery and danger, which undoubtedly included the shadow beasts—departed almost as soon as I arrived at the Tower. The vines I traveled by were strange to the touch at first. It had been many seasons since I had swung in the forest. Far below me, Kip and our team seemed small and sluggish. I was flying again!

As the City faded behind us, the tree limbs grew closer together and visibility became difficult as leaves clogged the area closer to the ground. I dropped to the dirt and waited for Kip.

"I can't see through the dense leaves," I told him. "I'm not sure where to go."

Kip's calm demeanor didn't change. "Where do you *think* you should go?"

I felt as if he wasn't listening. I tried again, with more force and animation: "It's too thick for me to see up there."

Kip sat on the ground and called the team around him. He asked us, "What is our mission? We are seeking new sources of maize, right?" We nodded. He continued, "Indeed. Now, why do you suppose I chose each of you?"

"Well," I said, "you picked me because I can swing in trees and help guide the—"

His interruption startled me. "If that is what you think, you are not the leader I hoped you were," he said. That embarrassed and confused me—I had expected affirmation. Fortunately he didn't let it hang in the air very long. "You are a monkey and capable of swinging on vines. However, I had no knowledge of the forest we would face. I didn't know if I could use your ability to swing through trees. I needed an innovative thinker who embraced challenge. That is who I understood you to be."

If I had been wearing my work vest, the buttons would have popped off. Inspired now, I wanted to scale that tree and get back to work, but Kip continued, reviewing one by one each member's strengths. He had chosen the two protectors for their unique and unwavering courage, not necessarily to defend the team from assault. He counted on them to maintain our motivation and focus. The cook was certainly skilled with a pot and utensils, but also brought compassion and caring which Kip quickly called out as a critical component to success. The hoofed animal was as sure-footed as he was patient. Kip had chosen him for his calming disposition.

Then Kip stood, smiled, and said, "Each of you is a key ingredient in our recipe for success."

It was already evening, so we decided to camp there for the night. He completed his remarks with something he called *The Recipe for a Healthy Community.* In my mind, I imagined it in the format of mom's recipe book.

RECIPE for a Healthy Community

Respect the ingredients*:

- Ingredients of a community are the *passions, feelings, skills, failures,* and *successes* each unique member brings.
- Demonstrate *respect* for yourself and community members. This is the base of the recipe.
- *Empathy* allows us to understand and respect each unique perspective.
- *Wisdom* finds balance to regard differing views equally.
- Whisking together combines individual experiences into a unified vision.

Encourage others:

- Meet members in the emotion of their choosing.
- Positively create an environment for creativity, innovation, and expression.
- Embrace change as a constant.
- Adapt to change with words and actions of encouragement.
- Celebrate differences, promoting transformation.
- There is more than one successful way to mix ingredients.

Commit to the menu:

- The chef must create a menu that includes all perspectives.
- Appreciate the ingredients.

- The menu is a roadmap of what we will plate and how we will plate it.
- Some will order off the menu. Accommodations are always an option.
- Be willing to modify, but never compromise the integrity of the kitchen.

Practice what you plate:
- You must be willing to do what you say.
- Adapt while preserving the importance of each ingredient
- Use the same ingredients yourself that you require of others.
- Lead with fearless passion and tireless resolve for continuous improvement.

Innovate flavors:
- Innovation thrives when you eliminate boundaries.
- If a tree is in your way, incorporate it into your solution.
- Alter thinking, processes, and paradigms and you will find revolutionary concepts waiting to be tested.
- Never limit the kitchen to the vision of the chef.

Expect it to taste good:
- The staff is a reflection of the chef, emulating emotion, energy, and expectation.
- Believe in your team and they will reciprocate.

- Expect success before it is realized.
- Leaders trust their vision.
- If you document your recipe well, it will taste good each time you make it.

*Note: ingredients change with the environment

The wood burned brightly under the canopy sheltering us. It illuminated the darkness in a blanket of amber and gold. I peered across the circle we had formed and could see Kip's confidence as one who had lived and experienced success and failure in the kitchen of leadership. Back in the City, Jimmy was not following this recipe. My thoughts swirled with applications of Kip's wisdom.

The next morning, I climbed into the trees with new energy and purpose. As I reached the solitude of the leaves, I could hear ticking in my pocket. The disk's surface, when I drew it out, was smooth, and no plank protruded on which to write. Turning it over in my hand, I noticed a word, almost transparent, slightly visible on its face— *RESOLUTE*. The disk was reminding me of a strong truth of character and principle I had etched many years before. The side of the disk began to glow bright red. As I turned it, the glow nevertheless remained in the same position in my hand, as though pointing me in the way I should go.

Not until that moment did I realize the full value of the disk. Mom had called it the directional memory piece. Not only could it capture truths and recall them in order to help me along the way, now I realized it also offered guidance when I was unsure of the direction I should travel. Turning in the direction of the glowing edge, I returned it to my pocket and began to swing through the limbs.

Be resolute in your pursuit of this purpose, I told myself, just as my face emerged through the cap of leaves into the sunlight. I created a new way to soar above the foliage. Swinging below the cap, I gained enough speed to break through the canopy just long enough to maintain my bearing. I continued that way for most of the day.

———•—•———

Days passed. The approaching horizon seemed unchanged, but I was committed to finding a clearing or meadow that offered some hope of maize. Thankfully Kip and team kept me focused. My hands were now calloused and not as sore as in the beginning. My arms were growing stronger, as they had been in my youth.

I had just hauled myself above another patch of leaves when I detected the faint scent of smoke. I moved a little faster, thinking we might be approaching a community and the possibility of warm bread and a cooking fire. I imagined sipping steaming hot coffee with a new friend while spinning a yarn.

I encouraged myself aloud, "It must be just through the next bunch of leaves. Push harder!" I was traveling at full pace, so it wasn't long before I emerged above the canopy on one of my swings and found myself in a cloud of smoke, thick enough to irritate my eyes. But even though I couldn't see clearly, I sensed danger and grabbed a bare limb nearby and held on with all my might, stopping myself cold. I was listening to the dying echoes of a frightening sound before I realized that it was my own scream. Even before I was consciously aware of the danger, my body had responded.

There were no trees ahead. The ground had fallen away into a rocky crevice that faded into black as I tried to peer to the bottom. And the branch I clung to dangled over it.

Pulling myself back to safety, I tried to gather my thoughts. What was this? Where was the smoke coming from? And then I heard Kip's voice: "Hey, Pete, are you OK?"

I quickly slid to the ground. "There's a huge drop ahead," I said.

Within minutes Kip and I stood on the ground at the crevice's rim. "It's a canyon," Kip calmly replied. "We'll have to find a way around in the morning. It's getting dark. Let's make camp here for the night."

Later that night, I was still deep in sleep when nearby voices roused me. "What do you think it is?" asked a voice I recognized as our black-and-white chef.

Kip's voice, when he responded, held a level of concern and intensity I hadn't heard before: "The sun seems to be rising—but it's much too early."

I got to my feet and went to stand beside him, gazing at the odd glow to the east. Our minds must have worked at the same pace, because by the end of the few seconds it took me, even with my mind still addled by sleep, to put together the persistent smell of smoke and the glow on the horizon, Kips suddenly shouted, "This is fire!" It must have been huge, because just like a sunset it seemed to engulf the entire width of the skyline. A steady breeze blew the haze of smoke across our campsite, predicting the dangerous path of the inferno. We packed our gear, and then the team huddled as he gave us our directions.

"We need to get word back to the City and warn families in the Town and the Community," Kip said. Then he sent the protectors to the Town and the Community. "Pete," he continued, "Swing as fast as you can back to the City and warn Jimmy. I'll follow on the ground with the gear."

I left immediately. Dreadful thoughts filled my imagination. How would I tell the citizens of the City this news? Instead of maize, we found potential extinction. What about Ellie, the kids, Mom?

The thick smoke kept me from swinging at first, so I ran on the ground. Finally, the odious cloud lifted. Soon I was flying again. But with every catch and release came thoughts of disaster and fear. Unpleasant visions of the future flashed before my eyes. How much time did we have? Would the blaze leap the canyon? How would I explain this to Jimmy? I braced against a solid tree to gather my thoughts, sensing that I was becoming slightly hysterical. I desperately wanted to turn south first and save my family. Sweat formed on my face as I wrestled with my options. I knew what I should do, but my emotions told me otherwise. I calmed myself with a few deep breaths. And in that moment of stillness, I heard the soft ticking of the disk. I had been too busy this morning to check on it. When I retrieved it from my pocket, another word was revealed on its side, and once again, the glow of direction. It read RESOLUTE PURPOSE. The disk was encouraging me to continue in my task. *Back to the City.*

It seemed like an eternity before I made out the outline of buildings. I had stopped only briefly for sleep on this journey, and I was exhausted. After resting on a branch, I dropped to the path and entered the massive mountain of glass and metal, trying not to cause alarm, even though I must have looked a mess. It was midday, which crushed any chance of secrecy. And to my surprise and confusion, I found that anxiety in the City had worsened since our departure. Citizens bustled about in a frantic rush. What if, in their agitated state, they panicked at my news? Could my message itself prove to be more dangerous than the prospect of a forest fire?

Despite my stealth approach, word spread that one of the team had returned. They didn't know which team member, nor did they know why I was alone; however, that didn't stop them from speculating. Rumors reached the Tower before I entered its gates. Ronald greeted me as if I were an outcast. With eyes of stone and without a word, he opened Jimmy's door and led me into the office. I could see only the backs of several heads. It was clear that the leadership team was in a tense meeting. Other than Jimmy, who was speaking about shortages and protests, none of them spoke.

Jimmy took a measured amount of time to recognize me. "Where's Kip?" he said, and I heard more fear than anger in his voice. "I hope you have good news." Stepping to the front of the room, I started to explain what we had seen when a thunderous sound stopped me mid-word. Ronald plopped down in a chair and regarded me as if he were about to sentence me to death. The other leaders quickly exited the room. I could only assume that Ronald wasn't understanding what I was saying and what danger it put the City in, so I continued, speaking this time with more intensity. I made it to the part of the story at which Kip gives me my instructions to rush back to the City when Jimmy slammed his hands on the table.

"Enough! This is the most absurd story I have ever heard!" he crowed. "You expect me to believe that we will all be consumed by a fire?" He rambled on in the same vein, saying nothing about what must be done to save the citizens of the City from the fire and mostly expressing his strong view that monkeys are not good for much of anything. I had been a bad choice for this mission, he said, and I had failed. He gave me no chance to speak again. Instead he offered me a choice: "Leave under cover of night," he said, "or face public humiliation." Jimmy's face made it clear which I should choose.

Ronald escorted me out of the Tower, assuring me that he would see to it that Jimmy announced how I had betrayed my team by leaving them alone in the forest and abandoning our quest in cowardice.

I sat down just outside the Tower. I couldn't think. I needed to control my emotions. I was angry and overwhelmed. I had known it wouldn't be easy to bring this message to Jimmy, but this was not what I'd expected.

"Why did you direct me here?" I shouted, grabbing the disk through the fabric of my pocket. "How could this be my purpose?" *How could he accuse me of such treachery? I would never betray Kip and the team!*

Eventually, calm prevailed, if only because I still had loved ones to save. I opted for a shameful exit and snuck out under the cloak of approaching darkness. Sharing the details of the imminent catastrophe with Ellie would make it easier to bear. She always made things better. She made *me* better. I couldn't even risk going to Herman and Jo's place to explain it to them; I had been banished. They would be so upset.

I had sat there longer than I'd realized. As I crept in the dark past the city square, the large screen came to life. Jimmy had wasted no time. There was his image, complete with an annoyingly fake smile and look of arrogance.

"Citizens, I have news," he began, "The search party has made progress. They are still searching for maize. They passed the darkest part of the forest and sent their scout back with an update. He quickly returned to rejoin the quest. We will continue to ration supplies while we prepare more storage sheds for more maize." Cheers filled the streets as the anxiety I'd sensed earlier morphed into excitement. I looked around me. The citizens believed him. They were inspired.

I could take no more. I needed to get out of the City, but first I needed to chronicle what I had learned.

 Leadership is not synonymous with integrity or honesty. That is character. Powerful leaders can still be wrong and can still guide me in the wrong direction. Believe in leaders, but verify before I follow.

I took a final glance at the crowd. No, the anxiety and confusion I'd sensed earlier was still there, and perhaps that was the real cost of deception. The citizens appeared purposeless and sickly. Prodded by Jimmy's disregard for the truth, I snuck to the bins to see for myself. The primary bins were empty, as were most of the others. The hungry citizens in the streets were once again becoming noisy, and why not? Their bellies were empty. They were almost out of maize. Jimmy's remaining staff continued the charade, while citizens wandered dark streets with faces glued to MEVEDs, absorbing empty messages.

As I made my way toward the edge of the City, I noticed block after block that appeared to be no longer inhabited, or at least only sparsely so. Anywhere was better than this tomb. I wanted to shout out about the fire, but I knew the message would fall on deaf ears. I remained cloaked until I got out of the City.

Ellie was a welcome sight. The protector had arrived, carrying Kip's message, and the Town leadership was still in session, formulating a response to the crisis. Ellie and

I decided to take our family back to the Community. I spoke with Jay and Emma, offering to take them and their family with us, but they declined. "We belong with the Town, and we will stay with them. Be safe, friend," Jay said. Ellie and Emma cried, hugged, and said goodbye while I packed the family's essential goods—or at least all that we could carry—and the remaining harvest of maize.

Within a few hours we were ready to cross the Hedge— and I was surprised at the guilt I felt that it had been so long since I'd been back to see Mom.

Chapter Eleven

Mom's smile washed negative emotion away like a warm bath on a winter's night. When I told her about Jimmy's ruse and the plight of the remaining citizens, she remained calm, grabbed my hand and said, "You need to see this." She led me at an uncomfortably fast pace, and I was surprised at how much faster she was moving than before. Behind her home, a bazaar of animals popped in and out of tents and up and down in carts. Everyone was working. I could hear hammers striking nails, saws cutting wood, and the clang of pots and pans. I was dumbfounded. It was an incredible sight.

Mom's best friend, Kay, appeared at her side. "Welcome home, Pete," Kay said, her voice warm and familiar. "Where's the family? Are you hungry?" I was famished. And tonight's dinner turned out to be one of my favorites, made only here in the Community. A warm mound of vegetables and fruit, wrapped in thick flat bread. My childhood favorite.

Over dinner, I learned that Kay had moved in to help as Mom's new vision began to take a physical toll on her body. Kay was so much like Mom. She had grown up near us and had helped care for Dad when Mom and I were unavailable. She had a large family of her own, but had always found time for us. She had even helped raise me, though I rarely admitted it. I loved Kay like family.

I was overwhelmed by the welcome from everyone in the Community. I had been gone so long, yet everyone showed me the same respect they gave my mother.

I sent the family to get some sleep, which left me alone with my thoughts. I wrote in my journal.

 The feel of our Community has a depth and weight similar to that of the Town of berms. The City's vastness and impersonal pace creates a much different culture, a self-serving culture, in contrast to the Community's atmosphere of unity. Because of the City's weak foundation, the fear of fire will consume the citizens well before the flames reach the City.

The next day, I walked through the multitude of animals now surrounding Mom's home. It resembled a military compound. Neatly organized into sections, it was a labyrinth of bodies and tents. Strolling past a group of young animals, I heard a familiar voice but couldn't see through the mass of fur, paws, and tools. There was serious learning taking place. I stopped a hustling builder as she scurried by and asked what this was.

"It's the learning tree," she scolded, as though everyone should have known.

"Who is teaching?" I was almost afraid to ask.

"That would be Dr. Dale," she said, her voice now fading away as she ran on. I pressed through a gathering of young animals and stood on a log. I could just see his face. It was Dale; he had made it to the Community. As it turned out, he was originally from the Community and now shared his vast knowledge with anyone who would listen.

I was also happy to learn that Herman and Jo had returned a while back. When I asked about them, I was told that they were down by the crushball field. That was no surprise, but what I found at the field stunned me. Instead of crushball, lines of strong animals were working in tandem, marching in cadence, learning formation drills, and mastering the defensive arts. There was Herman at the front of the group, training alongside the others. It was impressive to watch. I felt much better knowing that Herman and Jo were also safe and back in the Community.

I realized that Mom had been planning this for some time. All of her cryptic messages had pointed to this. She had a vision, and Kay was helping her put it together. Family and friends had arrived from near and far to fulfill her plan. I just didn't yet know what that plan was. It was time for another serious talk. But first, I had learned something I needed to add to my journal.

The Community has learned to grow REAL fruit through transparency, equality, and trust.

- Respect your community and yourself
- Encourage others along their path
- Assist all who are in need
- Listen with unbiased objectivity

I decided to skip the coffee for this discussion. I needed to look her in the eye and get to the facts. As she approached, I could see by her walk that she was in pain. A grimace accompanied every step. She was laboring just to get to the yard. The past years had taken more out of her than I had realized. I rose to help her and was met by that stare of determination I knew so well. It was the same determined stare I'd seen in Dad.

Kay almost sprinted past her with a pot and two cups. "It's tea," she said with a chuckle. Mom explained that she had changed drinks to help with her stomach. No coffee after noon.

"Then tea it is," I said cheerfully, hoping to brighten the mood. Only later did I realize that she didn't need it. I got right to the point. "Mom, I need to know what's happening around here. I don't recognize the place."

Her voice was tranquil as always. "I'm so proud of you, Son. Your determination and courage inspired most of the animals you see here. They know of your journeys and the risks you were willing to take to save the City. The protector shared it with us." She put her arm around me and pulled me close as she continued. "I taught you about faith, family and fellowship, roots that draw deep, wide, and far to sustain our community."

"I know, Mom, and the disk is helping me now."

"Son, you have been actively engaged in the fourth root on your journey, and I want to be sure you understand." Her countenance had become serious again. "Your recent challenges, hardships, victories, and defeats have all been in pursuit of sustainability. Food is the fourth root of our community and leadership tree. This root is used to maintain knowledge and resources that sustain us over time. It represents work, not wealth. We work to feed the community, not to define our self-worth. Working for the good of the entire tree provides harmony."

Even as she still spoke, I could see that I'd had it all wrong. I had been chasing work wherever I could find an opportunity to challenge myself. I remembered the teams at CNC, and how their community had grown through the joy they found in everything they did while working. I would need much more thought to fully understand this, but already I could see that the root of food is an integral part of my life, etched on my heart.

I hated to interrupt, but the need was urgent. "What about the fire, Mom?"

She spoke softly. "When you were home last, I pointed to the horizon and told you we needed to prepare for what is to come. You couldn't see it then, but intuition told me there was danger coming. That's why I began the Help Center. This band of misfits, as you call them, are from our community and beyond. They began to believe in my fortification and preparation efforts. Change is not easy to accept. It can be uncomfortable and intimidating. I began this center in hopes of providing protection for all in need. We started small but grew quickly in light of the impending danger. With so many animals congregating, we had to add temporary living space. They began to rally around the vision. Our numbers multiplied, requiring us to become more organized. We placed a lit torch at the top of the tallest tree so others could find us. It worked at first, but eventually wind and rain extinguished the flame. Some members built a small house and hoisted it up the tree to protect the torch, allowing it to burn day and night. We call it the lighthouse, and it's a symbol for what we do here. Many have come seeking refuge at this lighthouse. I teach grace and mercy while loving your neighbor so we can live in peace as we face the dangers approaching. We live in harmony with animals from all walks of life. Some time ago, as one of the congregation was replacing the torch, she saw a dark cloud to the east. Others ascended and realized that this was no ordinary cloud. Even before the protector arrived with the news, we knew that unless we acted, we faced certain destruction. We began building carts and wagons to transport family, food, and shelter. Our Help Center became a life raft.

"Beyond the dangers of the forest, there is a river. So we are preparing to travel west."

I shook my head, feeling very small. I stood and left her with a final comment: "Someday you must tell me how you seem to know things before anyone else. But right now, I need to know how I can help you."

"Walk among the tents, watch, listen, and learn," she said before retiring for a nap. "Then you'll know."

It was mid-day, but the sun was hidden behind dense clouds that reminded me of the looming peril. Ellie and I toured the rest of the Help Center, which was alive with laughter and the sounds of children at play. It was like a family reunion. Everyone welcomed Ellie and me back to our home. The families assembled around the Help Center were packing wagons and organizing for the long journey ahead. "Beyond the dangers of the forest, there is a river," Mom had told them, and they had believed her. "So we are preparing to travel west." I didn't fully understand it—how did she know the river was there? But I knew Mom, I trusted her, and I knew she had a plan. So I was here to help. I pitched in.

I'd been at it a few hours when Henry, one of my friends from school, came swinging into the yard like a lightning bolt. He had news—big news. He found the wide body of water to the west. I hadn't seen Henry since we were young monkeys in school. In the meantime, he had become one of Mom's most trusted friends and supporters. He had organized the building and loading plans, and now he sat and drew a map of the path to the water. It would be a dangerous trip, but it offered safety if we could find a way across the water.

As I stood at Henry's shoulder, watching the map take shape, I felt someone come alongside me. A voice I knew well asked, "Do you think there is maize on the other side of that river?" I got one of those sideways grins, turned, and offered my hand to Kip. He let out a chuckle and shook my hand. "Great to see you, Pete!" I was delighted to see him, but shocked as well. He updated me on Jimmy and the citizens. Chaos had been consuming the City well before the fire. Jimmy had hidden my reappearance and announcement about the fire, but when Kip returned with the same message, it ignited a full panic. The streets teemed with animals—those, at least, who had not already fled because of lack of food—frantically reading their MEVEDs to learn what to do next. Fact was overtaken by rumor and rumor confirmed as fact. It was pandemonium.

Jimmy, Kip knew, had a secret team prepared to lead him westward in search of refuge near the water while Ronald continued the pretense that all was well. Citizens kept checking empty silos, hoping in vain for food. PAWs ran astray in barren fields where overproduction had left little trace of maize. The message "ALL IS WELL" continued to broadcast on MEVEDs, leaving many animals in their homes quietly holding on to false hope. Communication was difficult because the reduction in maize harvests had eliminated much of the spark.

When Jimmy actually departed the City in secret, word was slow to spread. Ronald posted one final message of empty reassurances, then departed himself to join Jimmy's caravan. By that time, smoke from the approaching fire was wafting across the City square. Panic escalated with every eye-watering, choking breath—they had been lied to! Fire was imminent! It was foolish to remain in the City now. When the fire reached the power plants, all spark and communication ended, replaced by a tsunami of terror and desperation. Citizens who had not made independent decisions for years, or even generations, found themselves without leadership. Some locked their doors, refusing to accept reality. Others denied the truth and went about the City (stepping around dormant PAWs) as though they were busily completing tasks that no longer had any significance. A third group raced out of town without any sense of direction and no plan. The Tower had fallen.

Kip had made the decision to leave the City before he delivered the horrific news of the fire to Jimmy. He had concluded that finding me and the Community was where he needed to be. I was relieved. His skills would dramatically improve our chances of survival.

Sleep wouldn't come that first night, and I stared into the darkness. There was so much to do. I reflected on Dad and what he had taught me during our time together in the trees. Those trees would soon be ashes. It was all so overwhelming.

Mom's whisper penetrated the silence. "Join me on the porch?" Her voice was a welcome reassurance.

The night was calm, with a faint hint of smoke in the air. I wished I could believe it was from a large pile of leaves in the middle of the forest that my children had gathered for a bonfire, but there was no denying dreadful reality. Mom surprised me with two cups of steaming satisfaction, saying, "Some conversations just need a good cup of coffee." I loved her laugh. Dad had always said that is what he would miss most about her when he left this world.

Then she became serious again. "Hearing Kip describe the City's betrayal by its leadership reminded me of something very important." Her voice gained intensity. "We built this community on a strong sense of unity of purpose, valuing integrity, but most importantly forgiving those who had wronged us. Your stories, Son, are filled with a sense of anger, as though you want vindication. That is not how we lead. The fifth and final root of the community is actually not a root at all. It is the amalgamation of all roots through forgiveness."

"I'm not angry," I replied defensively.

"Son," she said. There was a long, intense pause accompanied by piercing mom eyes.

"OK, maybe I am angry, but I didn't deserve being treated like a liar and coward."

Leaning toward me, she calmly asked, "What can you control?"

"Only myself." I quickly looked away.

"When others cause you pain or change your course, it's not wise to simply sever the relationship. That is not good for the root system. You must find forgiveness in your heart and then, together with the one who wronged you, grow in common ground."

"Mom, it's not the mistakes of others that concern me the most. I should have seen through Jimmy! I should have known. I have made so many mistakes. How can I mend what I have helped to break?"

"You start by forgiving yourself. We are all fallible. *Forgiveness* allows *faith, family, fellowship,* and *food* to sustain a healthy community." She leaned back in her chair with a look of finality. "You have matured in your journeys. Looking at your own weakness is always the best path to healing. You are ready to lead."

I felt encouraged, as if this was a final lesson, and I had passed. Her eyes were growing tired, but her spirit was bright. I kissed her on the forehead, "What would you like me to do next?"

"Take your place by my side and help me lead this group to safety."

It was already first light, and the sound of busy workers could be heard. Mom walked me through the construction areas, explaining each piece of the puzzle. Carts and wagons were lining up. Canvases draped hoods of protection over their valued contents. Vegetables and fruit were diligently checked and prepared: quick brushing, light hosing, thumping, squeezing, and determined sniffing to detect ripeness. Quality was paramount to sustainability.

I was amazed at each step's simplicity: reduced to its most elemental process and repeated masterfully.

The functions were as standardized as breathing. Some lines grew long while others retracted, as they met the fluctuating demand for bristle, bottle, and seal. And thus food was prepared for the journey ahead.

I quickly wrote in my journal:

 Optimizing production requires simplified and standardized processes that allow workers to move between tasks with ease while maintaining the integrity of the work.

I left Mom and walked further down the path. There were colorful leaves randomly plastered to the sides of wagons. Then I noticed similar leaves on necklaces and even on hats. They all bore writing of some kind. I stopped a worker wearing one around her neck. She had long ears and a big smile. Her name was Hope, which was quite fitting.

When I asked her to explain the leaf, she said, "I was caught in the act."

"Caught doing what?" I asked.

She seemed a little surprised that I didn't understand. "Caught in the act of doing something good. Kay started giving these awards when we began our work here. But anyone can give or earn one." She pulled her necklace off and handed me the leaf. It was faded, almost illegible. It read, "Hope was caught in the act of doing something good. Thank you for helping the kitchen staff with the dishes." Hope, now beaming, said, "It happened late one night. My own work had ended and I was out for an evening stroll when I came across the kitchen staff, still hard at work because they had fallen behind on dishes. They would never have asked me to help after I'd spent a long day on my own tasks, but I was glad to jump in and help them finish. The next day, Kay presented me with this leaf. That's how it works."

These leaves, I saw, were an authentic recognition of important things, whether big or small. Celebrating others for doing the right thing was a small thing to give, but such a big thing to receive.

The ticking disk in my pocket caught my attention, and this time, when I pulled it out, it released a plank for me to write on. I added *AUTHENTICITY* into the welcoming flames.

On my way back to Mom's home, I met a large group approaching from the direction of the Hedge. Right at the front, smiling and waving, was a familiar face: JB. Jay and Emma were behind him, followed by most of the dwellers from the Town. Our numbers were growing daily. And although we varied in many ways, our cavalcade was united in purpose.

Mom called the leadership teams together. She had created a group of wise community members from every clan. Mom was at the helm, and each leader had an equal voice. After she called the meeting to order, she added JB, Kip, and a few others, and then introduced me as the expedition leader. I was shocked, but not surprised. This is what she had been preparing me to do. She stood on a stump so that she could see everyone and they could see her. Her right hand rested at her side and she loosely gripped a long stiff root in her left. The root was dry and firm and slightly taller than she was. Mom had wrapped the end of the root to give the appearance of an open hand—symbolic of many things, but it made me think most of the five roots of our community. Although I was sure she had much to say and little time to convey it, she took a moment to look over the group.

Then her voice fell across the crowd. "I see many here who have labored for months on these preparations, and others who have just arrived. All will share equally in the journey. You are welcome here. Our growing numbers are equaled only by our spirit and desire to survive.

"And survive we must. The flames of death are nearly at our borders, and the time to move is now. We have separated you into groups, each with a specific and valuable purpose. Our path will be difficult, and many will be tempted to doubt along the way. Some may fall away from the road and call you to join. When that happens, you will know that they are not seeking the path to deliverance. Our path requires faith and discipline. Trust yourself and your neighbor. Whether large, small, fast, or slow, we survive together because we are a community."

With a gentle tap on the stump, she was off.

In truth, her plan was more sophisticated than her message had implied. There were three groups. The forge team would advance first, moving slowly, choosing a safe path that would allow the wagons and animals the easiest trek possible. The main body would follow, protected by the third group, the protectors. I would be leading the forge team, with Kip at my side. Mom had warned us of dangers in the forest ahead. Since childhood, I had heard stories of large dark creatures with extremely sharp teeth and ferocious appetites; now it appeared that those stories were more truth than folklore. I thought of the shadow beasts and hoped we would be safe in the light. My scouting journey with Kip had taught us both much about what we should and should not do when scouting. The forge team consisted of a scout team and an excavating team. Swift advance scouts would run the forest floor ahead of my team and report back to all groups. The monkeys would stay with the larger group, sweeping trees on either side and to the rear. That was where Henry would be with our trained marchers at his disposal as the protectors.

Herman would lead the main body. Mom, Ellie, Jo, and Kay would be at the front. JB and Dale relayed and interpreted reports from my team of scouts for the main group, so that the group could adjust their strategy as needed.

My forward team included five hundred small but rugged earth-moving animals, the excavators, from all over the forest who would clear and shape a path for those who would follow us. We had miles of unknown terrain to prepare for the feet and wheels of the main group. *I must be decisive and diplomatic,* I reminded myself.

It was time to depart, and my newly formed team of earth-movers was as tense as it was diverse. Developing them would require intuition and insight. Without development and support, this team could quickly dissolve into disorder. I tried to snap them to attention with the voice of command I had spent hours practicing. "You are one group now, not simply individuals. I will call you the Dozers," I said. My goal was to unite all the animals into a cohesive unit behind a new name, but their soft, nervous chuckles told me that, as yet, I hadn't achieved that goal. Then my disk began to tick. Quickly retrieving it from my pocket, I hoped to find a word of inspiration to share with the team, since I couldn't think of anything to write or say in this embarrassing moment. In the light glow of its face were the words EMPATHY and HUMILITY, and the disk's glowing side clearly pointed west. But I couldn't release them to begin their task before I was confident that they were ready. I looked back across the sea of fur and tried to see the situation from their perspective. *They must be afraid. And certainly, they don't yet have any reason to trust me.*

Clearing my throat, I tried again, this time with less bravado and more respect. "This journey is as dangerous as it is necessary. I don't know about your life, I don't yet know your story, but I know that the Community is counting on us. I promise to give you everything I have, to listen to your ideas, and to work together to succeed."

As I made eye contact with one of them after another, I could see their belief began to build. "I ask you to put your differences aside and join me as Dozers to clear a path to safety."

Chants of *"Do-zer"* confirmed that our group was now connected through our devotion to the cause. And I was their leader now.

Kip, of course, I had known for some time, but one major member of my team was new to me. Saul was my scout leader. He had sharp horns and was fast and strong. His physical prowess had earned him his spot by my side. Everything about him was majestic. His role was retrieving information from the field scouts and executing my orders. His squad of field scouts looked like him, only slightly smaller. Saul and his scouts pranced around the Dozers with gallantry. They had little unity, but they understood and respected each other's role. Anything out of balance was reported immediately to Saul, Kip, and finally me. Kip would stay with the excavators, providing direction to the Dozers. Their entire focus was heads-down work, creating a smooth wide path. I had led teams before, but always under the watchful mentoring of someone else. This undertaking fell solely on me.

I found it ironic that once again Kip was by my side, only this time our roles were reversed. With his example to guide me and with his unwavering support, I was ready to direct. I made a note in my journal acknowledging the respect he showed me.

Confident leaders bestow respect and endorsement on the ones they develop. Encouraging success through others is oftentimes more rewarding than personal accomplishment.

The scouts dashed into shadows of the thick forest, and we were on our way.

Chapter Twelve

Time passed quickly. We were conscious always of the threat approaching behind, reminded by the smoke and ash that swept over us from time to time. We were slightly ahead of the main body but received sporadic word of their progress from the scouts. My scouts returned from their explorations only long enough to pass an occasional message to Saul, then they were off again to the darkness of the trees. They covered expansive swaths of forest but now, more than a week into our journey, the forest was so thick visibility was difficult. One tree folded into another, creating a wall of bark. This slowed our progress immensely. My diggers often felt they were digging straight up tree trunks, whichever direction they turned, and yet we were charged with creating a path adequate not just for foot traffic but for wagons. I was becoming concerned about the health of my Dozers. Saul's scouts were returning much more frequently now—apparently, they were not searching far ahead. I pulled Saul aside and asked whether he was satisfied, and I was surprised by how nonchalant he seemed.

"Nothing to worry about," he grunted.

I asked a few more times over the next couple of days, and each time he repeated casual, almost dismissive reassurances. I would have to trust him, but the less communicative he was, the harder trust became.

We were moving slowly through the forest. Extremely so. And yet the exertion and strain were taking a toll on my Dozers, so I called for a day of rest. The Dozers were glad to finally have a much needed respite, but Saul seemed distracted, almost preoccupied. I assumed that was because we were now more vulnerable, which would naturally make him worry. He wandered away from the group frequently, and when he was with us, his eyes seemed fixed on the dense forest ahead.

A scout rushed into camp, seemingly alarmed. He delivered his message to Saul in an undertone, let out a soft but frightening squeal, then immediately vanished through the forest walls. I had heard that squeal before—from a family of deer mired in the mud many seasons ago. They had been frightened. The scout must be as well.

Saul froze as soon as he received the message. He simply glared at the trees and didn't respond when I asked what was happening. The fur on my neck began to rise. The next scout flashed through the underbrush, but I leaped in front of him and clutched his antlers with both hands. Looking him directly in the eye, I said, in a fierce voice, "What is happening?" I didn't want him to hasten away like the last one without knowing why they were so frightened.

"I have to report!" he hissed.

"You report to me!" I hissed back.

There was a brief standoff, and then reluctantly, he gave in. "Most scouts have left their posts. Saul instructed the remaining scouts to double the size of our zones and report more often."

I was alarmed. "We sent twelve scouts into the field. How many are still roaming?"

"Four."

This was dreadful! We had dug our way far enough into the forest now that we were exposed to real danger—and we had almost no scouts? My feet barely hit the ground as I ran to Saul.

"What is going on?" I shouted. I was still waiting for his reply when I caught a glimpse of a shadow slinking just beyond the tree line. I acted as though it wasn't there and softened my voice. "I need you to return to the troop and warn them." One shape became many as their profiles became clearer, revealing sharp teeth and thick black coats. "Shadow beasts," I whispered. But it's daytime— they should only come out at night." I could now see the familiar yellow eyes. They seemed to look through me.

"The smoke must be pushing them out of the shadows." I reached behind me to get Saul's attention, wanting to make sure he was seeing what I was seeing. I found only air. He had already bolted, streaking to safety through the trees. I climbed a vine as fast as I could, all the while knowing that the Dozer songs my crew was singing were calling to the beasts like a dinner bell. I shouted and screamed, but the shadow beasts paid no attention to me. Too far away to help, I could only watch as the dark intruders encircled my team. With Saul gone and with me high in a tree, it was just Kip and the Dozers on the ground, now aware of their danger and drawing into a tight bunch, back to back. It was as though I was watching through the screen of a MEVED. A hush fell over the entire group. Kip's eyes glared as he snarled and showed his tiny sharp teeth. He was a valiant, fearless fighter, but he was no match for these larger creatures. His coat would soon be covered with a different shade of red. I was too far away to swing down and pull him to safety.

Not waiting for the shadow beasts to attack, he launched himself at them. His bravery was captivating as with blinding speed and quick, evasive turns the beasts couldn't match, he bounced between them and wove among the bushes and trees. He seemed unaware of the danger he was in. But the beasts were too many. His last glance was at me, seemingly to say goodbye. Then he was gone—the shadow beasts cut him off from the rest of the Dozers and then took chase, pushing him deep into the trees.

Only minutes later they returned. I knew that they would now turn their attention to the hundreds of defenseless Dozers. Like me, the shadow beasts had temporarily lost interest in them as they pursued Kip, and I had swiveled to the opposite side of the tree to try unsuccessfully to watch the beasts' pursuit of Kip. Now I turned my attention back to the Dozers—and noticed for the first time the mounds of dirt where hundreds of small brown bodies had once quivered in fear.

Kip's attack and flight into the forest had been a diversion. He had offered himself to provide an opportunity for the Dozers to dig their way to safety. All that remained in the clearing was a frustrated, salivating pack of angry beasts and a good lesson in strategy.

 I learned two valuable lessons in leadership today. The courage of selflessness and the indignity of selfishness. Kip was willing to sacrifice everything for those who needed him the most, while Saul thought only of himself. His self-centeredness clouded both his judgment and his perspective. Kip's unwavering commitment to the team gave him the strength to execute his plan and allow his team the time to find safety. Saul vanished into the darkness, losing his majesty, dignity, and respect along the way.

I reached for my disk just before it began to tick. **SACRIFICE** belonged on a plank.

A day later, the larger group arrived, bringing safety with numbers. Kip—who, remarkably, had managed to elude the shadow beasts once he had led them far enough away—and I rejoined them as the Dozers began to emerge from their makeshift bunkers. We had lost our advance scouts, so travel was more deliberate now, with guards posted within shouting distance of each other. According to our map, the water was close. And indeed, within a few days, we walked gratefully and joyfully into the open terrain leading to the river's bank.

It took a few days for our community to assemble along the shore. The water was swift and rough, although it didn't appear to be impossible to cross—just difficult and dangerous. It was cold but clear enough to see about one average monkey's tail into its depths.

We had outpaced the smoke, which afforded us time to rest and plan. Mom pitched her tent near the water. I sent the leaders to organize their groups, then return for a strategy session. We needed a plan before we attempted to cross. We met in a circle near Mom's tent, which was easy to identify because she had placed her root firmly in the ground before it.

I took a minute to add to my journal.

The image of a hand atop the leadership root is a symbol of unity in community and of leadership through faith, family, fellowship, food, and forgiveness.

The leadership team met for a long time with no agreement on how to cross the threatening water. After all, there were young ones, small animals who didn't swim, and wagons laden with the supplies we would need to make a new life for ourselves on the other side. But with the smell of smoke came the realization that we had no choice. We must cross.

Across the river, I could see fields of the familiar stalks of maize beckoning me, almost as if they were mocking my journey.

A young hoofed animal just a few feet from me pranced to the water's edge and stepped in. He tested each step carefully. When his stomach touched the water's surface, he began to thrash in a panic, apparently trying to turn back. The water around him was bubbling now. He made it out of the water in two leaps, then fell to the ground in a moaning heap. There were small tears on his legs and stomach that appeared to be bites.

An undercurrent of murmuring spread all around me now, as the news spread that swimming the river wasn't a viable option. Standing at the water's edge, I could see thick grass swaying in the current just below a tail's depth. Whatever had bitten the young animal remained sheathed in the river grass; I could see nothing swimming. I decided to call them deep river biters.

Mom remained confident that we would still cross the river. In fact, she was packing her tent when she called me over and asked me to search further down the river for a possible place to cross.

I headed downstream. The trees didn't grow as close to the water here. Soon I could hear voices, and I caught glimpses through the trees of hurried movement. When I got closer, being careful to stay hidden, one familiar voice caught my attention. It was Jimmy. Some of his group had made it to the river as well. There appeared to be no more than two hundred citizens. My heart hurt for those who weren't with us. Lost to the fire? Still scurrying frantically to find safety? Many of them had been my neighbors and co-workers in the City, people I had liked and respected.

A large group was attempting to build something out of trees—just what it might be, I could not yet tell.

Moving even closer, I could see that nothing in leadership dynamics had changed. With Ronald at his side, Jimmy was squawking orders in every direction. It was complete confusion, yet Jimmy continued to sit on his elevated throne as though he owned the river.

Don't overlook the value of your team. The best ideas often come from unlikely perspectives. It may be a Dozer, a Scout, or another animal working in the field. All animals have value. A true leader takes time to listen and values the input of others. The shortest distance between two points may be a straight line, but the smartest distance usually includes other points.

I withdrew, still undetected by anyone in Jimmy's group, and made it back to our community, pausing briefly to watch Ash play with the animals from different groups. Their friendship reflected the importance of community. This was worth recording. I looked for Mom and was told that she wasn't feeling well and had moved upstream. She had taken only a small group of animals with her and had asked that she be left alone. That worried me. Should I check on her? The disk in my pocket was ticking, so I pulled it out—it was glowing in the direction of the citizens. I decided to respect Mom's request. I had one more task to complete. I had been writing in my journal more frequently now. It was the best way I could think of to pass my knowledge on to my children.

 Character is developed through grace and tested in the fire of diplomacy and moments of solitary leadership. I must extend a hand to compromise with those who ridicule and even reject me.

The next morning I traveled downstream again. This time, I could hear music and laughter coming from Jimmy's group. I decided to ease my way in and offer a hand of friendship. I glanced to the east; the smoke now filled the sky in that direction. I tried to clear my head before entering their camp. Dancing animals bounced around me. Jimmy stood on a log with a satisfied look as if he had just eaten the last banana.

He quieted the crowd and spoke confidently. "The fire is upon us, and we will now launch this bridge across the water, securing it on the other side. After we cross we must destroy it to keep inferior animals from following and consuming our maize." The crowd cheered.

I knew I was not welcome, but I climbed to a limb on a nearby tree so I could be seen. I cleared my throat "Excuse me—Jimmy?" No one reacted. I was about to shout when Ronald looked up, recognized me, and silenced the crowd. "Can I have your attention? Quiet down! We have a visitor, or should I say the lost scout has found his way back," he said with a belly laugh and obvious sarcasm. "Pete, what is it that you have to say?"

"I hope your bridge is successful," I said. "I have a large community of animals just up the river. We traveled here together and are now trying to find a way to the other side. I would like to bring them down to cross your bridge before you destroy it." Before I had finished that final sentence, the jeering was so loud I'm sure no one heard me.

Jimmy jumped off the log, pointed at me, and shouted. "We don't need your kind in our new city. We will rebuild better than ever and keep all the maize to ourselves. Go back to your community and tell them they are not worthy to be citizens. Now leave!"

He didn't have to tell me twice. I grabbed a vine and safely swung into the nearby forest, where the smoke was already thick enough to provide cover for my shameful exit. But once I'd moved far enough away from Jimmy's group, I settled on a limb with a view of the river and rested long enough to watch the launch of their bridge. Citizens proudly rolled the mighty wooden structure over logs toward the river. When the bridge reached the water, citizens jumped on the bank side, lifting the front above the water's surface as if it were a lever. The bridge slowly moved forward, hovering above the water.

But somewhere about halfway across, the launch became problematic. The animals providing counterbalance, as the portion of the bridge still on land grew smaller and smaller, were increasingly crowded, inhibiting their ability to advance the bridge. There came a tipping point, when they had a chance to pull the bridge back and reconsider, and several voices could be heard calling that idea out, but Jimmy stood on his stump shouting the same command over and over again: "Forward!"

And so the team pushed ahead. The front of the bridge began to lower—but too soon; it was still several tail lengths short of the far shoreline. One timid worker jumped off the bridge, and the retreat began. Bodies flew into the air as the giant wooden structure plummeted into the water. The power of the current was remarkable in this part of the river, even more swift than where our group was still gathered upstream, quickly making mulch of their hopes and aspirations. An appalled hush fell over the citizens. I didn't wait to see how Jimmy reacted, but I could hear it in his voice as I swung back toward our community.

There was frantic activity near Mom's tent. Most of the community seemed to be gathered there. Ellie was waiting for me. "You go ahead," she said. "I'll join with the kids soon." I took off. It was hard to find a place to step, the ground was so full of animals. The air was abuzz with stories of death and disaster. News had traveled from the forest. The fire was close. We were sandwiched between flames and the teeth of the deep river biters.

Mom was in her tent when I arrived. As soon as I pulled the flap back, I could see that she was not well. Mom never stayed in bed this late in the morning. I noticed water steaming in a pot over the fire outside, so I poured us both a cup of coffee. I found a comfortable seat and leaned close to check on her. She looked at me with the love only a mother knows.

"I am so proud of who you have become, Pete," she said in a weak voice. "Now I have much to share, and time is short." This sounded like goodbye. My throat tightened even more. I did not want to hear the rest.

"Don't be afraid," she said. "This is what you were born to do. This is your purpose." As weak as it was, the sound of her voice still warmed me.

Ellie arrived and sat on the ground, settling against my leg.

Mom patted me gently, then continued. "When you were a baby, I knew you were special. You noticed things and asked questions most animals didn't think to ask. What really separates you is your enormous compassion and empathy. Your intuition has always been sensitive to the needs and gifts of those around you. You developed your purpose in life over miles and hours of training and testing. Along your path, you have met strong mentors, great friends, and leaders you prefer *not* to emulate. Your character is derived from all of that. Your greatest resource is sitting on the ground at your side. Ellie is a gift, guide, and guardian. Don't lose sight of that. Hold tight to her. Together you are stronger."

My tears stretched from eye to chin now, because I knew that this was the end.

The ticking in my pocket temporarily interrupted the moment. As much as I wanted to ignore it, I also thought it might be important. I took the disk from my pocket and pulled out the plank. Then I asked the question I would never again be able to ask her: "What should I write?"

"Think of the five roots," Mom said. "Each is more valuable when you share it with others." She extended her hand toward me. "Keeping your faith to yourself, rather than sharing it, withholds from others the promise of hope. Refusing to love your family unconditionally restricts the blessing of kinship. Restricting fellowship weakens the community. Stockpiling food limits community growth. Withholding forgiveness hardens your heart." Her hand was now clinched into a fist. "You can't lead others with a closed hand." She relaxed her fist into an open palm. "You must always extend it graciously with your gifts."

The disk beckoned me again. This time, I handed Mom the disk, with plank open. She wrote **GRACE**, smiling at the blue flames as if they were the oldest and dearest of friends.

"You have written important life and community notes in your journal," Mom said, "etched powerful leadership characteristics in your disk, and engraved the key community roots on your heart. Today, I need to share one final principle. We cling to five truths, five roots that make up the foundation of our community. A strong community embraces everyone equally without distinguishing between ability and wealth. We do not judge appearances or opinions." She gestured toward the root stuck in the ground near her tent's door. "I lead holding that root to remind me that we are joined through the five principles." She reached into her bag and retrieved something small, which she kept hidden in her hand. "You see the connection? Build on your faith, love your family, encourage fellowship, work hard to provide food, and foster forgiveness to bind everyone together. That is community. Now, I have something to show you." She opened her hand, revealing a disk much like mine but much older. "I have written in my disk for years, since long before you were born. And even up to today, I have continued to learn from it." She pulled onto her bed the beautiful dark reddish wooden box with deep carvings that I had first seen on that long-ago day at her house, when I had first received my disk. Mom pulled a plank, about half the length of the ones I had written on, from the top of her disk. The edge was grooved on both sides. She inserted it and opened the lid. I could see older disks inside as she quickly removed a note and the tapper she had shown me long ago. Sealing the box and handing me the note, she said, "Don't read this until you are in the middle of the river. You still have much work to do."

Now, surprisingly, her voice became stronger, as though she were gathering her strength to give me one final direction. "Go to the water's edge and trust your instincts. Take a step of faith and fulfill your purpose." With her weakened arms, she handed me the shorter plank and quietly whispered, "I have etched for the last time." My tear-filled eyes focused on the face where she had etched **MERCY**. I inserted her plank into the newly opened space on the top of my disk. It became warm as the face glowed brightly on the side facing the river, the direction I must now go. As my eyes lifted from the disk, Mom's fell into eternal sleep. I realized she was handing me the key to the box and my future. Mercy integrates all I had learned into our community and my leadership.

Pushing the flap open, I could see the sun somehow penetrating the smoke-obscured late morning sky. It created a portal directly to the heavens. I called the leaders together and told them of Mom's passing. The mood quickly became reverent. Despite our need to outrun the fire, using some river-crossing method we had not yet discovered, we committed the time to respectfully lay her to rest. I spoke of how she saw the beauty in everyone and mentioned the help she provided with no regard for personal cost. She never knew a stranger and welcomed all to her table, leading by example in word and deed. I placed on the ground a plaque that read, "Raye, beloved wife, mother, and friend—the embodiment of grace and mercy in the face of adversity." Ellie and the kids were at my side. What a legacy.

There was so much to say, but we had work to do. It was time to face the river. Grief and mourning would have to wait. I looked across the water at the maize. I almost resented it now—and at the same time, I could almost taste it.

JB appeared at my side. "Yesterday," he said, "your mom had a small group of animals cutting stones and leaving them in harnesses. That's why she insisted on being left alone. For hours, she worked at the water's edge. I could hear her singing and occasionally splashing in the water well into the night. She spent all of yesterday with her handpicked workers. This morning she asked for you just before you arrived at her tent."

I felt sad that I had not been with her during that last day. But I couldn't dwell on that—I had to understand what she had been up to. The fire was upon us and I needed to act. The sun was now setting, enhancing the fire's glow. I walked to the water's edge where Mom had been working. Dusk was descending and I could see myself in a new light now. My task was heavy, yet my confidence had grown. My purpose had brought me to the steps I would now take. With my throat closing and my vision blurred, I looked back at Ellie, the kids, and thousands of animals gazing at me just behind them. Kip, JB, Oliver, and Herman were ready to jump to my rescue, but I knew this was a passage I must make alone. A cold breeze froze my breath as I looked across the water. Embers of fire extinguished themselves on the surface, announcing the arrival of our final chapter. I recalled the five roots as I looked at my mom's root, her staff, now resting in my left hand. Drawing on my faith, I stepped into the water.

It was cool, but not cold. I could feel every bubble, twig, and stone, but no bites. At least, not yet. The risk was in the depths to come.

Looking to the sky, I whispered, "I believe," and stepped forward boldly to my destiny. My steps were still shallow as I moved further into the river, which was odd. Why was the river not growing deeper? Somehow I was not sinking. Now I had reached the middle of the rolling water. Confused, I turned to see the shoreline I had left behind. No one had moved. All eyes were on me, and everyone looked as confused as I was.

I pulled Mom's note out and began to read in the glow of the flames.

My Dearest Pete,

While others were racing around looking for big ideas, I stayed calm and simplified the problem. As I told you, everything grows from its root— including problems. You must identify the root cause of your problem before you can solve it. Our problem was the river bottom. Its depths allowed the mysterious river biters to reach us. The solution was to raise the river's bed. I did that in the shallowest part of the river, using the stones chiseled by our community. I worked with only a few team members because sometimes even simple solutions prove too difficult for everyone to understand. You must address challenges one rock at a time. I enjoyed my final hours of labor— knowing that I was providing steps to your future renewed my strength. This rock surface is wide enough for every cart and animal to cross safely. When you reach the other side, carve what you have learned on the box. You are their leader now. I am so proud of you.

I love you infinity.

Mom

I stood in the middle of the river for a while and let the tears flow. Then I looked back at the shore and saw Ellie. I'm not sure I touched a single stone as I darted back to the bank. I raised my voice and explained to all about the rock surface, then I asked the leaders to station animals along the edges of the underwater pathway with torches to ensure safe passage to the other side. Then I urged the animals to cross, and they began to do so immediately. They lifted their voices in joyous song as they walked past Mom's root/staff, which I had planted alongside her pathway a few feet beyond the water's edge.

It took most of the night to safely escort every cart, tent, family, and heirloom across the water, but by the time the sun began to rise in the east, my task was complete, although I had not yet crossed myself. I looked up and down the shoreline to make sure we were leaving no one behind. The fire was hurtling toward the river, pushing heat, smoke, and an eerie glow ahead of it. As I turned to follow Mom's path to freedom, I discovered to my surprise that I was not alone. My family was still standing at the water's edge, waiting for me.

"What did you mean on Grandma's gravestone when you said 'grace and mercy in the face of adversity,' Dad?" Ha's voice reminded me of mine many years earlier.

I thought for a moment, then smiled and said, "Follow me, and I'll show you. But we must hurry." My heart swelled with pride as my wife and kids jogged with me along the shore. Looking across the water to where nearly all of our community now awaited us, I could see Ash as he played with Oliver in safety there. *My family is my legacy too,* I thought, and to me it seemed as if the shadows of the five of us represented the five roots as we rushed along the riverbank on an important mission: to offer safety to the arrogant citizens who had been willing to destroy our hope of survival only hours before. This was the right thing to do. It would bring the balance we needed in our new community.

Many from Jimmy's group followed us back to safety, but Jimmy, Ronald, and some others rejected our offer and chose to move further down the river's bank to find their own path to safety.

I was the last to reach the protection of the western shore, and no sooner had my foot settled onto the sandy bank than I paused to write in my journal.

 The only thing I can control is my actions. I can offer assistance to others, but they must be willing to change themselves. My role is to try to influence culture through grace, mercy, and truth while remaining open to feedback. This ensures continued growth on my journey. A leader must rise above personal feelings and do the right thing, even when no one is watching.

From the safety of the western shore, we cheered as the fire reached the water—and simply burned itself out there. All that we had left behind, all that we knew from our previous lives, was gone now, burned to cinders. But we could begin again in what appeared to be a rich land.

I climbed to a hilltop in the middle of the field of maize and watched as our community made camp in the beautiful forest. They had already begun rebuilding their lives. We had balance now. We had water, a forest for shelter, and maize.

I sat and pulled out my disk. Everything I had engraved there reminded me of the journey we had just completed. I relished the sight of my family walking across the golden field with Hope by their side. Pulling the tapper from my pocket, I began to carve on the box. "We're going to be OK," I said, amazed that I could say that after all we'd faced. When the carving was complete, I placed the tapper and sketcher back in the box.

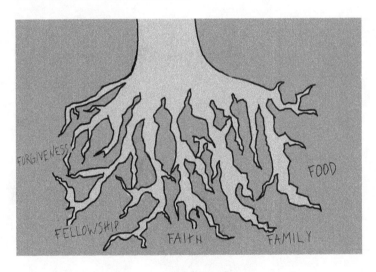

Leaning back on the gentle slope, I gazed into the sky. The sun warmed my face as a peaceful calm filled the air. Closing my eyes, I could smell freshly brewed coffee as plainly as if it were in my hand. Comfort and warmth refreshed me. I heard methodical tapping like that of my disk, calling like a distant drum. A damp cool touch fell across my cheek.

"Want to talk?" the voice was familiar. My hand reached to wipe the moisture from my cheek and found the gentle muzzle of Libby welcoming me to a new day. The room was bright now, filled with new morning's light. Sitting up, I saw two cups of coffee in Ellie's hands. It was clear to me now. The answer to my problems would grow from the five roots of community and from life with my Ellie.

Conclusion

A Word From the Author

My story is still being written. Ellie, now in full remission, holds her cup next to mine. We crossed our river together bridging the roots of faith, family, fellowship, food, and forgiveness with these principles –

Purpose	Encouragement
Empathy	Resoluteness
Service	Relationships
Influence	Humility
Integrity	Sacrifice
Authenticity	Mercy
Grace	

I encourage you to reflect on them as you grow your life with the truths of this book.

S. Mosby Marble

Acknowledgments

I am most grateful for God, my creator, as my faith is my anchor, my comfort, and my hope. I know I can do all things through Christ.

First, I thank my amazing wife, Elaina, for countless hours of reading, listening, and advising me as I shaped this story over the years. She always kept me balanced and knew when to push me and when to just give me a hug. I am glad she never let me follow through when I said I was done. This story began in my heart and developed through my relationship with my Ellie.

My children are my universe, and I owe a special thanks to each of them:

My daughter Chenae Marble for early edits, story revisions, countless hours of reading, and the painful conversations when I just couldn't understand her point of view. Thankfully, she persevered until I understood.

My daughter Alora Moore for her unwavering support and words of encouragement but especially for extended time in her prayer room. She lifted me throughout this process. She also provided my technical support for graphics and creative designs.

My son, Steven Jacobi-Ha Marble (Jacobi), for inspiring me to be my best self and to never give up. He listened to my repeated stories as though it was the first time he had heard them. His ability to see the good in everything and everyone inspires me to be a better person every day.

My son-in-law, Brandon Moore, for his creative talent and perspective on leadership and community. He made time to discuss leadership concepts and design ideas while working and completing his graduate degree.

Writing a book is harder than I thought but incredibly gratifying. It would not have been possible without my publisher, David Hancock and Morgan James Publishing, who believed in this story and in publishing my work, and my editor, David Lambert, who realized my vision and had the patience and talent to take a first-time author and shape my writing into a story.

I have been very fortunate to know Dick Robinson. My many years under his leadership developed my love for reading and made me a lifelong learner. Thank you, Mr. Robinson, for your commitment to literacy, learning, and my development.

A heartfelt thanks to Jennifer Duncan, Deanna Price, and Becky Williams for being my support group for more than two decades in leadership. We cleaned numerous floors and served thousands of employees together. Also to my Virtual Band of Brothers and Pinnacle Forum

Leadership group, who supported me with counsel and encouragement, and Dr. Johnny Parker for sharing his experience and skill as an author. Thank you, Aly and Sheila Weber, for sharing your talents and time in design and creative decisions.

About the Author

S. Mosby Marble is a lifelong entrepreneur and
corporate leader. He completed his undergraduate degree
while owning a small business,
then transitioned to the corporate world while completing
his MBA. Marble has served
in a variety of leadership roles
in the community, including
school board president, church

deacon, and community services board member. In the
business world, he has held positions ranging from general
manager to vice president in fields from customer service
to human resources to operations. He spent over twen-
ty-four years as a senior leader for Scholastic Book Publishing and Charter (Spectrum) Communications. Marble
is a Christian who finds his purpose in the teachings of
Christ, expressed in both word and deed. He wrote *The
Monkey and the Maize* as a tribute to his incredible par-

ents and his amazing wife. Marble and his wife have three grown children and reside in Jefferson City, Missouri.